Journeys into the Heart

by
Drunvalo Melchizedek
and
Daniel Mitel

Balboa Press books may be ordered through booksellers or by contacting:

Balboa Press
A Division of Hay House
1663 Liberty Drive
Bloomington, IN 47403
www.balboapress.com
1 (877) 407-4847

Cover copyright: Editura For You
www.editura-foryou.ro
Editing & Interior Design: Demetra Teresa Tsakiroglou
www.heartmindsynergy.com
Imagery of Mandalas: Zlatko Kanda
www.zlatkokanda.com
Image of Magnetic Field of the Heart: HeartMath® Institute

Print information available on the last page.

ISBN: 978-1-5043-7498-9 (sc)
ISBN: 978-1-5043-7497-2 (hc)
ISBN: 978-1-5043-7496-5 (e)

Balboa Press rev. date: 02/20/2017

Table of Contents

Foreword

Never in the history of the human race has there been a more important time than now to understand and embark on the journey into the heart. The conversion from the heart to the brain that took place thousands of years ago, has cost us dearly. Learning to go back into the heart is not just a spiritual matter but, under the given circumstances, it might be the essential thing to do if we wish to continue our life on this planet.

Although, long ago, living in the heart used to be our natural state of being, this has been lost over time in the intricacies of the ego; we have forgotten what it is like to be free, to fly. From the Sumerians to the Tibetans, from the Indian Saints to the Holy Fathers and Holy Mothers of Egypt, there have been generations of people who had dedicated their lives to practicing the ancient methods of living in the heart.

You may think that it would be necessary to move to the Himalayas or to Tibet in order to practice these ancient methods; that living in the busiest city of the world prevents us from practicing these exercises or that it is necessary to have a Master to guide us into our heart. The Master, however, who is authorized to guide you into your heart is the spirit behind the eyes reading these words now. That is you. You are now empowered to do it. You have the ability to do it.

Read and enjoy practicing and applying all the methods in this book. Decide the appropriate one for you.

Then practice, practice and practice again and remember who you really are.

Finally, read about our experiences of going into the heart, about the prayer of the heart and living in the heart. You might find them very helpful on your own spiritual journey.

Remember: You and I are alike. I am you and you are me.

Drunvalo Melchizedek
Daniel Mitel

Drunvalo Melchizedek

Chapter 1

The Unity Breath Meditation

One thing that indigenous people of the world have taught me is that before any important ceremony, one must connect in love with Mother Earth, then with Father Sky and ultimately, through this experience, with the Great Spirit, or God. It is no different when one is about to enter the sacred space of the heart, otherwise this space remains elusive.

I had originally learned what I am about to tell you in 1981 from one of my Taos Pueblo mentors, Jimmy Reyna, and knew it in a very simple and unrefined manner. But here enters one of the great spiritual teachers of the Kriya Yoga traditions, speaking in elegant terms.

I was about to go on stage during an event called "The Solar Heart" on Jekyll Island, Georgia, in about 1994. Several spiritual teachers were taking turns to lead the audience into a higher and higher unity with Spirit. I was to be next. I was behind the stage in a small back room sitting before a meditation altar where someone had placed a single lit candle and a set of photographs from the Self-Realization Fellowship. There were pictures of Krishna, Jesus, Babaji, Lahiri Maharshi, Sri Yukteswar and Yogananda.

I knew that before I had to actually go on stage, someone would come and get me, and I already knew what I was going to speak about, so there was nothing left to do but to center. For me there is no better way to do this than to enter into meditation.

I acknowledged the teachers for the greatness they are and closed my eyes to begin meditating. Slowly the world around me began to fade into the distance, and as the energy began to increase, I had a vision. This single moment altered the course of that evening with the audience and later the course of almost everything in my spiritual world.

Within a short time, Sri Yukteswar appeared to me with a noble expression on his face. Though I have had a close relationship with Yogananda, Sri Yukteswar's disciple, I had never really thought about Sri Yukteswar himself. But there he was. He went directly to the point, as I will now.

He told me that, in India, no one would even consider approaching the divine without a certain state of mind and heart, and he gave me very specific instructions on exactly how to consciously connect to the divine and finally with God. Here is what he told me.

You can be anywhere, but I use an altar with a single candle to focus my mental attention. I feel and know the presence of my teachers, and we all begin to breathe together, as one.

"Let your attention shift to a place on Earth that you feel is the most beautiful place in the world. It could be anywhere - a mountain scene with trees, lakes and rivers; or an arid, sandy desert with almost no life - whatever you perceive as beautiful. See as much detail as you can. For example, if your place is a mountain scene, see the mountains and the white, billowing clouds. See and sense the forest

and the trees moving with the wind. See the animals—the deer and elk, little rabbits and squirrels. Look down and see the clear water of the rivers. Begin to feel love for this place and for all of nature. Continue to grow into this space of love with nature until your heart is beating with the warmth of your love.

"When the time feels right, send your love to the center of the Earth using your intention so that Mother Earth can directly feel the love you have for her. You can place your love into a small sphere to contain it and send it to the Mother if you wish, but it is your intention that is so important. Then wait, as a child. Wait until Mother Earth sends her love back to you and you can feel it. You are her child, and I know she loves you.

"As your Mother's love enters your body, open completely, allowing this love to move anywhere throughout your body. Let it enter all of your cells. Let it move throughout your lightbody. Let it move wherever it wishes to move. Feel this beautiful love your Mother has surrounded you with and remain in this union with Mother Earth until it feels complete.

"At the right moment, which only you can know, without breaking the love union with your Mother, look to your Father, to your Heavenly Father. Look to the rest of creation beyond the Earth. Place your attention on a night sky. See the Milky Way as it meanders across the heavens. Watch the planets and the Moon swirl around you and the Earth. Feel the Sun hidden beneath the Earth. Realize the incredible depth of space.

"Feel the love you have for the Father, for the Divine Father is the spirit of all of creation, except the Divine Mother. And when this love becomes so great that it just cannot stay inside you any longer, let *it move into the heavens with your intention. Again, you can send your love into the heavens inside a small sphere, if you wish."*

Sri Yukteswar says to place your love in a small sphere and with your intention send it into the heavens. He says to send it to the unity consciousness grid around the Earth. If you do not know what this grid is, then do not worry. Just do as most of the indigenous peoples of the world do: send your love to the Sun. Like the grids, the Sun is connected to all the other suns or stars and eventually to all life everywhere.

Some people, such as the Hopi of the Southwest of the United States, send their love to the Great Central Sun, which is another concept that not everyone has but that is equally valid. Choose one — which one does not matter. The intent is for your love to reach all life everywhere.

Sri Yukteswar continued: *"Once your love has been sent into the heavens to the Divine Father, again you wait; you wait for the Father to send his love back to you. And of course, he will always do so. You are his child forever, and the Divine Father will always, always love you. And just like with the Mother's love, when you feel the love of the Divine Father enter your being, let it move anywhere it wants to. It is your Father's love, and it is pure.*

"At this moment something that rarely happens is manifesting: the Holy Trinity is alive on Earth. The Divine Mother and the Divine Father are joined with you in pure love and you, the Divine Child, complete the Triangle."

According to Sri Yukteswar, it is only in this particular state of consciousness that God can be known directly. And so the final step in this meditation is to become aware of the presence of God—all around you and within you.

For this part of the meditation, Sri Yukteswar had originally given me a very complex way of being aware of God, but after speaking with many elders of various tribes around the world, I feel we can simplify the way to reach this final state of consciousness. It really is simple:

Once you are in the Holy Trinity, you can achieve this experience by simply opening your heart to the presence of God. For some reason that only God knows, in the Holy Trinity state the presence of God is easily perceivable.

Sri Yukteswar gave me the name of this meditation: the Unity Breath. God is always everywhere, but humans do not always perceive God. The Unity Breath meditation takes you directly, consciously into God's presence.

For some, this state of consciousness is all that is necessary to complete all cycles created by life, or in another way of saying it, it is the doorway to approach all the sacred ceremonies of life, such as our birth into this world, sacred marriage and even death. According to the Native Americans, even the ceremonies of planting and harvesting crops require this particular connection to Great Spirit for the crops to grow and be healthy.

The natural way is to co-create with God, or Great Spirit, to assist in the cycles of nature to bring balance to life. According to the Bible we are the keepers of the Garden (or nature) as described in the story of Adam and Eve, and in this modern time we still are, but we have forgotten our purpose. Without this inner connection with God we are separate and lost, hence this meditation of Sri Yukteswar is the opening to remember God and to enter and remember the sacred space of the heart.

At this point, Sri Yukteswar became very stern. He looked me straight in the eyes and said, *"Drunvalo, 1 want you to go out onto the stage today and teach the audience this meditation I just taught you"*. He looked at me like he really meant it, and I thought I'd better not disobey him. Then he bowed and disappeared.

I remember hearing the knock on the door that told me that it was my turn. I remember getting up, confused. I did not know what to do. I'd had a plan as to what I was going to do and say, but this seemed to override everything. I told the stagehand that I would come along in just one minute, closed the door and quickly brought in the angels. They advised me to do as told by Sri Yukteswar, that eventually I would understand. And so I did, and so eventually I did understand. Once I was out in front of the audience I told them what had just happened and that we were about to enter into a meditative state that Sri Yukteswar had strongly suggested we all experience.

I led the audience through the steps while I followed my own words. Then there was silence, and bliss. A long time later I was pulled out of the meditation by a young man tugging at my sleeve and telling me that we should be ready to go to lunch in ten minutes. Everyone in the room, except those watching over the group, was deep in meditation. I asked people to slowly return, but for the first time in my life I found many in the audience who were so deep into the meditation that they could not or did not want to come out of it. After several attempts to retrieve everybody, there were still about thirty people who just did not want to return.

We sent people to them individually to get them out of their meditation, and all of them eventually did come out - except one young man who we thought was going to have to be taken to a hospital. After maybe twenty more minutes, while everybody else was eating lunch, he finally opened his eyes. All I could think was, "*What happened?*". I had an experience that stayed with me beyond the meditation. I could still feel the love of my Mother and Father and the presence of God everywhere and in everything. It was delicious. It was beautiful.

Over the years I have learned to be careful with the Unity Breath meditation. Once one enters this state, one does not want to leave prematurely; it feels too good. So if you practice this meditation, leave ample time for yourself. Shut off the phones and do what is necessary to remain undisturbed with no time limit. Let the experience unfold like a summer flower. Now that you know the Unity Breath, always enter this state of consciousness first before you enter the sacred space of the heart. Otherwise, no matter how hard you try to find the sacred space, it will run from you; it will hide, leaving no trace.

Once you have reached the level of consciousness achieved by the Unity Breath, you may find that it gets easier and easier until, finally, you are in this place all the time. This is the ideal according to all of my mentors who know of this meditation. I believe that the Unity Breath creates the vibration within you that allows you to find the Holy Grail, the sacred space of the heart, the place where God originally created all that is. It is so simple. What you have always been looking for is right inside your own heart.

Moving within the Body

From the male point of view, there is movement associated with entering the Sacred Space of the Heart. Without this movement, the brain is only imagining you are within the Sacred Space of the Heart, and this is not true.

To be clear, from a female point of view, it is possible to simply change images. If you ever have the chance to enter one of my wife's workshops, Claudette Melchizedek uses this female method that is about 6,000 years old. Her work will expand what is learned here in this course, as experiencing from both the male and female way is desirable.

To understand why there is a movement, let me explain. Either you are in the brain or in the heart. It is one or the other. So you must leave the brain and move into the heart, and this is done by moving from the brain to the heart.

However, this idea of moving within one's body is outside of most people's understanding of themselves. Most people believe they are their body, and do not understand how they can move inside of their body.

Spirit, your spirit, can be either infinite or finite. If it is infinite, then you are the universe and being infinite you have no center. There is no place that is the center of the universe if the universe is infinite.

But your spirit can also be finite, as it is now. And being finite, you will have a place that is the center of your being. However, this place can be located within or outside of your physical body. For most people, it is located at this time in your Pineal gland or the Pineal chakra in your brain. But for other people their center is located in many other locations, such as their heart chakra.

A few people even have their center outside of their body. But it is almost always inside their Mer-Ka-Ba field, about 55 to 60 feet in diameter.

There are exercises that show you how to move your spirit. If you have never done this before, it may seem a little strange, but you will get it.

THE TORUS OF THE HEART

Chapter 2

Entering the Sacred Space of the Heart

The Kogi Way

The Kogi, an indigenous tribe living high in the mountains in Columbia of South America, had shown me a way of entering the heart space. They would go into a totally dark space and "dance" a slow movement that seemed to have no direction. They would continue this dance without food, water or sleep for nine days and nights. According to the Kogis, at the end of this dance, they would be in their heart space.

The problem with this way is that we, being the industrial humans that we are, are not strong enough to do this for nine days and nights. It is simply too difficult.

The Torus of the Heart

I then had to find another way and knew that the heart created a huge magnetic field in the shape of a torus about eight to ten feet in diameter (see image on page 14). It was believed that this field was generated by the Sacred Space of the Heart. I reasoned that if this is true, we could follow this field back to its source and find ourselves in the Sacred Space of the Heart. It works, and this is the first method that I had used. However, females have a hard time using this method. It is too logical.

The Way of Jesus

This way of entering the heart was first given to the world by Jesus. It came down through time by the Gnostic traditions. However, the Gnostics tried to hide this method from the public by saying that the Sacred Space of the Heart was not within the physical heart, but behind it. This is not true. But the entryway that Jesus spoke about is located behind the heart.

With this method, when you move from the brain to the heart, you move behind the heart and then turn and face in the direction you face when you are normally in your body. Now you are looking at the heart from behind. When you do this, you will see what looks like a crevasse or fold in the heart, and, in the middle of the crevasse, there is a small rotating vortex that appears either as a dark spot or a light spot. Move toward this vortex and, when you get close, the vortex will take you in, much like a vacuum cleaner, and you find yourself moving down a tube. Continue to move until you feel you come to a stop. At that moment, you are in the Sacred Space of the Heart. It is often referred to as the stillest place in the Universe.

The Pure Female Way of Intuition

This method is extremely simple, at least for females. For men it is a little difficult exactly because it is so simple. All you do is move from the brain to the physical heart and enter inside the heart from anywhere. Then with your intention, say to yourself that you are going to move and, when you stop, you are in the Sacred Space of the Heart. If you can use your female part of yourself, this is easy.

The Way of the Lower Heart Chakra

Though I know this is a very direct method of getting into the Sacred Space of the Heart, I have not been allowed to use it. There is a reason which is still not entirely clear to me. It has to do with multiple possibilities of where you end up, and I will not use it at this time until I know more about this method.

There may be other ways, but the ones we have do work. There are definitely female ways that have to do with imagery, and some of these methods are truly ancient.

Once you find your way into the Sacred Space of the Heart, regardless of how you will have arrived, it is easy to return there whenever you wish to. Just direct your intention of being there, feel the vibration, and...zap!... you are there in the holiest place within the Universe.

Chapter 3

Two Dream States

As almost everyone knows, the brain can dream at night while the body is asleep. But there is also a way that the heart can dream even while the body is awake. And so there are two entirely different ways or types of dreaming that are possible from within the human consciousness.

While asleep, the brain dreams, but these dreams are polarized. This means that the dreams can be good or bad. We can have happy dreams or nightmares. Of course we can have neutral dreams, because neutrality is part of polarization.

When we are in the Sacred Space of the Heart, the heart also dreams, but these dreams are not polarized. The heart is a unity consciousness and has no experience of polarization. Therefore, whatever it dreams, the dreams are only good. If you believe you are in your Sacred Space of the Heart and your dreaming is negative, you are not in this holy space. You are in your brain imagining you are in your Sacred Space of the Heart, and this is not real. This is still polarized brain dreaming. Negative dreams never happen in your Sacred Space of the Heart.

There is much more to this subject, since dreams that come from the Sacred Space of the Heart are more than what we normally believe.

Two Emotional Bodies

There are two entirely different emotional bodies in the human consciousness. The one that most of us are familiar with is generated from the right brain and it is connected to the Upper Heart Chakra. Since the brain is polarized, the same applies to its emotional body. We experience love, but we also experience hate. And each positive emotion has a negative emotion that is connected to it.

The Sacred Space in the Heart
Two Different Spaces

The Institute of HeartMath was the first in the world to discover that the heart produces the largest energy field coming from the human body, much larger than anything the brain produces, with the exception of the Mer-Ka-Ba itself. This magnetic field of the heart is in the shape of a torus, as mentioned before in this book. It actually has two tori, one within the other.

Metatron's Cube

If you have read about Metatron's Cube in Volume II of the book "The Ancient Secret of the Flower of Life", you will understand that it is one of thirteen systems of knowledge that creates the blueprint of the Universe.

You will notice the five Platonic Solids which create the details of the Universe and come out of Metatron's Cube also have a similar relationship to the two tori of the heart. You see the cube, and within this cube is a smaller cube. You see the octahedron, and within the octahedron is a smaller octahedron. The same applies to the other three Platonic Solids. This nature extends throughout the universe down to familiar relationships such as male and female. Though the larger contains the smaller, the smaller is the source of creation. The female contains the uterus, and this is directly connected with the Tiny Space of the Heart, the source of all things that exist.

The nature of the Sacred Space of the Heart is exactly like this. It has an outer space, which is the one always entered first, and then it has a much smaller space contained within the outer space that is usually found later. The second smaller space is usually very small, and, in the Upanishads, it is referred to as the Tiny Space of the Heart. We also refer to this smaller space as the Tiny Space.

The vibration of the Sacred Space of the Heart mentioned earlier is found in the larger outer space. Once you enter the Tiny Space of the Heart you will find that the vibration goes up in frequency instantly to what seems like a higher octave. You can actually move back and forth from the outer Sacred Space to the Tiny Space and hear and feel this difference.

Daniel Mitel

Chapter 4

Meeting the One

Know that the story I am about to tell is so important, that you might immediately understand the purpose of your life. Read it carefully and let the information flow through you, just as water penetrates the soil in quest of the small seed.

I have heard many predictions and stories about 2015, but nothing had prepared me for a meeting that took place early in October.

There had been a few interesting and intriguing months and days within that year's time. For me, an interesting and intriguing day exclusively and solely occurs during meditation. My daily routine consists of at least one long session of meditation, usually early in the morning, combined later with short sessions of prayer, Tai Chi, Qi-gong, Tibetan exercises and contemplative meditations. I also love exercising my body and, whenever I have the chance, I work out a little, especially with ab exercises and pushups on my fingers. Both sets of exercises greatly help me clean and activate the two main meridians from the spine and front upper body, as well as the twelve secondary meridians from the hands and legs. Of course, I also do a little bit of body stretching and mobility exercises for the muscles and bones.

In my effort to adapt my diet to my meditation time, it has simplified a lot. As I have written in my previous books, the Imagery Tibetan Masters had taught me about the power of the right food combination. The right food combination, in addition to drinking natural spring water, preserves the energy within the chakras and the meridians, making us feel full of stamina and positive vibration. One of the fascinating predictions made by the Masters has to do with the capacity of our body to absorb the enzymes from the food and higher vibration and energy of our cells.

More than twenty years ago, the Masters had told me that the period from 2015 to 2030 is referred to as "the years of liquids". This has to do with two very important changes that happen within the human body.

The first change is in the water that we drink. Our bodies will eventually and gradually reject more and more of the chemically treated tap water and the fake mineralized still water sold in supermarkets. If we do not have access to mountain natural spring water, then we need to find a formula in order to restructure the water we drink ourselves. In my workshops and especially in the "Heart Imagery" workshop, I teach some simple methods to restructure water.

The second change is in the food we eat. We need to eat less and less solid food and gradually increase our intake of juice and smoothies full of natural nutrients and antioxidants. Our stomach and liver cannot deal with large amounts of solid food anymore. Our body vibrations have become all the more higher and liquid food has become paramount in achieving a healthy life.

As a result, my diet has become very simple: a smoothie that I prepare myself after having finished my meditation in the morning and a plate of vegetables and olives in the afternoon. I have almost eliminated bread from my diet and have replaced it with powerful protein vegetable "goodies", such as avocado, quinoa, green peas, chick peas, beans, chia seeds, hemp seeds and a lot of nuts: pine nuts, macadamia nuts, walnuts, and so on.

I had gradually and slowly begun to incorporate these changes sometime in the beginning of 2015. They came to me in a natural way without analyzing or thinking why I had to do this. As I travel extensively around the world, an increasing number of people at my workshops, conferences and interviews have reported experiencing similar changes.

My diet provides me with a "light" way of living, so to speak. In combination with the right meditation or exercise, it gives me the clarity to see, sense and feel life at its highest capacity.

Watching over our Thoughts

Before describing the meeting I mentioned previously, I need to share some of the important findings and discoveries I have had throughout my spiritual life.

During my early childhood, I used to stare for hours on end at the trees in my grandparents' beautiful garden. I was aware of the truth, or should I say, I instinctively knew the truth. I had access to a gate of energy, a portal or a door that would open automatically and show me who I really am when I am in peace and harmony, in love and trust.

I rapidly realized that we live based on a set of belief patterns that continuously manufacture repetitive thoughts; thoughts of desires and wishes dictated by our egos. Years of education from three universities and numerous trainings proved to me that the majority of people live only on the surface of who they really are; their understanding and activities are, in essence, centered on their personal interests. Humanity has been continuously struggling to adapt to its own reality.

I carefully watched straight through the center of these struggles, the behavior of my family, friends, and people around me and realized that the activity of my mind is still part of my ego, regardless of whether the thought is positive or negative.

The first step in achieving the no-mind state is to focus on a specific mantra. The mental chanting of a mantra helped me for a while and I was able to clear my mind and center my attention on the primary thought given by the respective mantra.

But that was not enough. I quickly became aware of the fact that my mind had reshaped into a sort of a mechanical thing, closed and unable to see beyond the exercise I was doing. Something was missing from this spiritual activity. It took me a good many years to find out what the missing link was. I had to pass through all the world's continents and experience different techniques from ancient schools of meditation. I had to work with Masters of different spiritual schools before finding it.

The link is the heart. When we do not connect the mind with the heart, the mantra we chant is of no significance.

I had gone through different stages of understanding the path of awakening. If the mind activity was not the right one, then in what way could I progress in the course of my seeking God? Should I try the path of renunciation and reject anything related to this world? But then, would not all the lack of comfort, fasting, abstention and practice of restraining myself from enjoying anything around me turn me into a religious fanatic, missing out on life? Would not this be an act of violence against my own body?

I tried for a long time to understand the nature of thoughts. The words of St. Isaiah the Solitary resonated in my heart and in my spirit. This Mystic, who lived at Sketis in Egypt around the year 370 AD, had said that when we have an exact knowledge of the nature of our thoughts, only then will we be able to recognize those thoughts that trouble our intellect and make it lazy.

For me, this was of particular vital importance and I had to deal with it on a daily basis. Although my meditation time increased from an hour to four, even five, hours, despite spending periods of time sitting in complete silence, I still had to constantly push my thoughts out of my mind. Periods of deep meditation alternated and oscillated with bothering thoughts and memories. I desperately tried to send them away or keep them under control with my will power. A couple of times I even imagined a sword made of light, and whenever I had a thought or a memory, I would use the sword to knock it down and put an end to its existence.

Intuitively, though, I had the feeling that I was not doing the right thing. The solution was not to fight my thoughts; the solution should not be a violent one. Destroying a thought is barbarous and aggressive and, at its core, has the same energy as that of attacking and destroying anything else.

The solution was to transform the energy behind the thought, watching it with detachment, impartiality and open mindedness, instead of suppressing and controlling it.

My Years of Search

If mind activity would not help me reunite with the Infinite Spirit, then what would the best approach be in my arduous search to awaken my spirit? Should I choose the path of imitation? Should I focus all my efforts on copying the path of Jesus, or the paths of Buddha, Babaji and Yogananda?

Should I follow the exercises of the Tibetan Masters or the lives of Holy Fathers and Mothers, Mystics that lived almost two thousand years ago in Egypt, Syria, Cyprus and Greece? Or should I follow the path of the Persian Sufi Mystic Rumi with his famous spiritual writings that teach Sufis to reach their goal of being in true love with God?

I knew that the most important step was to catch the subtleties of my ego without identifying myself with them. All the years of search, meditation, reading hundreds of spiritual books would mean nothing if I was not able to meet my ego without fighting with it.

The Sufi Mystic Rumi would use the term "raw" or "men of externals" when referring to people who live without following any spiritual path. He used the term "ripe" or "men of the heart" when referring to Mystics and people who are on the path of God's realization.

Why did St. Augustine tell us not to look outside and to return to ourselves? He said that we must go within, there where the light of reason is enlightened.

Beyond all the spiritual advice and all the commentaries made by Mystics, saints and great Masters, I realized that a strong and powerful desire and will can train any mind to go beyond its conditions. However, a trained mind still continues to exist just as any other mind. Through my trained mind I was still unable to meet the Unknown.

Continuous years of search brought me to a clear conclusion: in order to enter the Unknown, I must abandon and give up all that I have learned from all the spiritual systems and schools, from all the Mystics and Masters.

My desires and efforts, my will and aspirations had not brought me the harmony and peace, the balance and beauty that *nirvana* promises. It did not even bring me to *nirvana*.

The only time I felt that I had really achieved a state of peace and freedom from any disturbances was in the moments when my mind was quiet, without chatter. I noticed that, when my mind was completely quiet, consciousness within me grew larger and larger into infinite proportions. My body and spirit would unify beyond time and space making the avoidance of any conflicting state and disappearance of my ego possible.

Surprisingly, I found this state of peace and harmony by utilizing only my attention. The key was a state of watchfulness and observance without interfering with anything that enters or comes out of my mind. I realized that this state of vigilance is *nirvana*. *Nirvana* is not a specific place and location, but a particular state of being.

This was a revelation for me in the sense that I realized two very important things. First and foremost, the Masters, the Mystics, the teachers and all the methods I had used until that moment of my existence had only served as a preparation before arriving to the real experience.

Secondly, and this is huge, I had to do it alone; nobody could do it for me. It was my job to do it. The Masters and the methods helped up to that point of my existence. It had to be *my* experience; not the experience of the Masters.

This opened me up to a completely new way of seeing things. I became fresh each day; I was a new person every morning when I opened my eyes. What Jesus had said about being reborn again became very clear to me.

I was living in Canada at the time and I would meditate each morning in my small garden, under a giant maple tree. Suddenly my life became so new, so fresh and full of presence like it had never been before. It was as if I had woken up from a prolonged and extended sleep.

There, sitting under my meditation tree, I would approach each event without any judgment or appreciation, without criticism or approval. I would just be there, doing nothing.

The revelation of doing nothing was very powerful to me as I was used to judging many things in my life at the time. Although I used to travel very often, teaching meditation methods to some groups all over the world, my main job was to manage a department at the Toronto International Airport.

I had to speak with hundreds of people each and every day. From a spiritual point of view I was literally in the middle of chaos and my revelation had a profound impact on my job.

I suddenly became conscious of my own automatisms; I was aware of all the actions I performed unconsciously or involuntarily.

I functioned like a part of a giant mechanism without personality and character. My charisma was pure ego.

Quickly and unexpectedly, I was able to shift outside this mechanism, able to watch its every move, without judging it.

Listening Beyond Duality

I learned to listen and see beyond the analysis of the mind. As the very function of the mind is to divide, fragment and analyze, whenever I was in a "no-mind" state I could develop another way of listening and perceiving the world around me.

I became able to listen as a whole, not just as a mind. Within this new process, I discovered another enjoyable feature: I stopped judging and analyzing the people who spoke, the words they would address to me or the actions in which I was involved.

Even when I had a desire, I would stop jumping for it. I would just consider it and then suddenly quit it. *Being* became my nature. *Being* is beyond duality. We are either in a state of *being* or in a state of *doing*. *Doing* is an achievement, a realization, a performance and a conclusion. We are consumed and conditioned by doing.

But *being* is something completely different. For at least three to four years after birth, we are in a state of being. We just are; we just live in the moment, we just enjoy the "now". Then we move into a state of doing; acting, willing, performing.

I literally felt as a child. I could listen to all the noise around me without interfering and judging it. I would be at work, right in the middle of the airport and feel as if I was in the eye of a hurricane. Surrounding me was the craziness of one of the busiest airports in the world and I did not mind at all. I was in that central spot of the hurricane where silence and peace abides. I could see, sense and feel the giant vortex of movement around me, but it did not affect me at all. I could clearly feel the perception that I am in the center of my being.

The only method I would use to stay in this state of being was intention and attention. Whenever I used my attention, I would be in a kind of perpetual state of motion; the energy that I would spend on anything I would do, would be replenished instantly with the same amount of energy coming from within me.

I would approach anything with this new method: the passivity of my mind and attention. Attention on anything without involving my mind, without criticizing or approving it, without any appreciation or denunciation. I would not censor, cut, delete or edit anything I watched. It would be just a simple process of seeing things without regarding them as pleasant or unpleasant.

I would suddenly be conscious of my automatisms and unnecessary repetitions. Through attention, I was able to sense that the performance of actions without conscious thoughts would begin to fade and disappear. Thoughts and images, desires and ideas, memories and resemblances, similarities and likenesses would become so rare, that they almost disappeared.

At this point, my negative thoughts would only appear when I did not apply attention.

It was an interesting way of encountering my self; pretty difficult, I would say. Thousands of thoughts would come and go in just a few moments under the pressure of my unbiased and impartial attention. There were instances when I could literally feel that I was empty. It was the taste of a new freedom; an unprejudiced and detached liberation of old belief patterns and systems.

The emptiness of my mind gave me an unprecedented boost of energy and freshness. A combination of vitality and liveliness, vigor and healthiness blossomed within me.

My friends, colleagues, family and students immediately sensed the change in my energy. The progressive practice of attention brought me quietness and a brand new state of abstaining from speech. Although my eyes would shine, full of light and energy, I would prefer to be quiet and just observe through attention. All the manifestations of my ego that would push me towards competition, ambition, control, dominance and superiority had begun to fade away and dissolve in the universal ocean of quietness and peace.

For the first time, just like an external observer, I was able to see a clear flaw and weakness in the structure of my ego. I had heard of stories about spiritual practitioners and God seekers, Mystics and Masters that had gone through a painful and long process, a hurting, tiring and exhausting fight with their ego. However, for me, the process was milder and more easy-going. The limitation of the mind, formed by years of conditioning, had broken down and had softly and gently disintegrated.

Inner Knowledge

More than four years had passed since I had first begun practicing the method of intention and attention. One very cold February morning, something happened as soon as I had woken up and begun getting ready for work.

The energy of the Canadian winters is amazing. There is a specific vibration in this part of the world in the winter time. You are aware that the temperature outside is minus 35 degrees, even though the environment is enjoyable inside. You are able to hear the quiet sound of the snowflakes touching the white coat of snow embracing the earth.

I used to wake up very early, usually at 3:30 a.m. and start the day with a three-hour meditation. On that morning, as soon as I had opened my eyes, I suddenly felt a powerful change in the structure of my thinking. Until that morning, I would wake up and watch the way my thoughts appear and disappear for a couple of minutes. But on that morning I was surprised to see that my thinking had changed its usual pattern. Effectively, I had stopped thinking. There was no mental activity at all; neither towards the past nor the future. I could hear the noise of the highway far away; I could feel the texture of the bed linings while in permanent contact with the present moment. I was in perfect unity with myself.

In this unity, an affectionate feeling gently began to manifest throughout my being. A consciousness of compassion, warmth, tolerance, sensitivity and tenderness began growing in me. I cannot compare or liken anything to what I felt at that moment of my life.

I left the house for work in that state of consciousness. I was unbelievably tuned in and adjusted to that specific moment. For a couple of hours there were absolutely no thoughts and the only thing I did was to be completely detached like an exterior observer that was looking at myself and at the exterior world.

I could clearly see myself and the people who were in contact with me as if watching a movie or a dream. The only difference was that I was able to consciously understand what I was doing; I was able to continue my actions without any interference from my ego.

I went home after work and got into meditation. In the meditation I could comprehensibly feel all my so-called values and sense of worth, all exterior behaviors and all the masks, leaving me on their own. This took place without my influence or intervention; it was a profound restructure of my mentality and reality. The only thing that mattered was the authenticity of my full presence in the actual moment; without any memories or thoughts of future.

All the relativity of the world disappeared and my mind was suspended in an empty hole, a hollow place, an opening that allowed contact with the "now", with the present moment. That state of awareness brought me to a new level of consciousness: an inner knowledge.

For the next couple of years I was able to see, sense and feel all the people around me trapped in their conditioned way of thinking and belief patterns.

I realized that the only way to get out of these repetitive gestures and structures is to correctly and honestly apply inner knowledge.

I also realized how narrow the path of self-knowledge is. The simple thought that we are on the path of self-knowledge is part of the ego's endless ways of keeping our mind and self-importance busy and occupied.

The Encounter

Nothing had prepared me for the encounter I would be about to have early in October of 2015. More than twelve years had passed since I had experienced an inner knowledge. It was not a doctrine, an ideology or a principle. It was a powerful and silent encounter with my Self.

Inner knowledge cannot be regarded as a method. It is an experience that comes when our ego stops functioning. It is a conversation with the Absolute, with the Universe. As soon as my ego became completely silent and inactive, I was able to open myself to the powerful gifts given by the Absolute.

I began that morning as usual: in my preparation for meditation, I do an advanced form of Tai Chi Quan, Yang style (85 forms), for half an hour and then mobility exercises for the spine and legs (Maha Mudra technique) combined with a little workout for my muscles. While I am not a yogi, before and after meditation, I particularly love doing Sirshasana, the headstand posture that increases the flow of blood in my brain and helps my pineal gland to clean out.

Sometimes, after meditation, I have an urge to lay down in Shavasana, the corpse pose. This exercise allows my body to regroup and reset itself.

I end my preparation for meditation and comfortably sit in a half lotus posture. This is my favorite meditation posture as when I sit on the forward edge of the small cushion, my spine becomes straight and my body is held steady for a long period of time after that.

Because of my extensive travelling, I do not have a particular favorite place to meditate; I meditate with the same intensity in any part of the world. However, when the weather is pleasant and agreeable, wherever I am, I really enjoy meditating outside, in touch with Earth and feeling the energy of nature all around me.

The island of Cyprus in the beginning of October has a heavenly fragrance. The sun rises early in the morning and the perfume of the flowers is unforgettable.

I went out in the garden in the delicate shade of a magnificent lemon tree, sat in my meditation posture and closed my eyes. My tongue automatically went into the Kechari Mudra position. I was completely relaxed and began to breathe rhythmically. Years of Kriya Yoga practice had completely changed my breathing pattern. As usual, after few minutes, a very pleasant energy completely surrounded my body.

Rarely in my meditations do I leave my body and move into the astral world. I generally move into my heart and have a "live" experience there. However, this time I felt a calling to move out of my body. I gently slid out of my body and moved softly up through the branches and leaves of the lemon tree.

I stopped for a moment and looked down at my body and, for the first time, without any hesitation, I placed my intention on meeting God.

An unexpected and incredible fast vertical movement ensued; I crossed a vast space, like never before on my journeys when I would leave my body. I felt that I was traveling through dimensions and universes, cosmic spaces and worlds. Billions of light years disappeared in just one moment and I passed through all matter and energy in the blink of an eye.

While moving, I was able to distinctly perceive certain profound noises, like metals scraping against each other and paper being cut by a sharp knife. That happened a couple of times. Each noise was associated with and accompanied by a clear feeling that I was shedding a cloak or a mantle that covered me. I lost count, but after the last noise, which was a very gentle and almost imperceptible sound, I had a clear feeling that I had shed all my bodies.

I became unlimited pure consciousness and cosmic light. I was a sparkle of light, lucid consciousness, that could move anywhere in the ocean of Infinite Spirit. An infinite number of similar sparkles surrounded me. Simultaneously, I could sense worlds and universes connected with me, the real me and all the sparkles around.

Time and space had lost strength. Millions of me, the sparkle of God, the primary intelligence of the Universe, had manifested in myriads of worlds, dimensions and spheres passing through my divine consciousness in a single moment. I was able to experience the "I am that I am".

Getting back into the physical body brought me a powerful inner silence. Even if I was in the confined space of the human body once again, I was aware of my contact with the divine me, with the primary thought of creation.

I lay down gently embracing Mother Earth, tears of gratitude flowing down my face. I became the oneness of man and nature, of man and infinity. I could feel the Universe within me; the whole Universe pulsating inside my heart. *I am that I am.*

UNDER THE LEMON TREE

Chapter 5

Lady Ana
The Great Avatar of Knowledge and the Intuitive Heart

In 1990, when I met Ana Pricop, I had a clear, spiritual routine. We loved calling her just "Lady Ana". She was so humble, modest and her earthly and cosmic moral codes and values were so high for us than even the word "Master" did not have any meaning when we addressed her.

In those days, I was regularly practicing Kriya Yoga and Zen meditation together with specific exercises from martial arts. At the same time, I read hundreds of books. I particularly resonated with Krishnamurti, Osho, Yogananda, Rumi and Carlos Castaneda's writings. I also studied five extremely important spiritual writings: "*The Urantia Book*", "*A Course in Miracles*", "*The Key of Enoch*", "*Mother's Agenda*" and "*The Philokalia*" which is a collection of texts written between the 14th and 15th centuries by spiritual Masters of the hesychastic tradition.

I had heard some stories about "the elderly Master woman" who could heal people by just speaking with them or who could teach people how to go into the heart with the use of certain powerful methods.

My interest to meet her increased twofold when a very good friend who knew her personally, told me that she was going to hold a conference very soon. I knew that she had a small group of students around her and that they were all working together on some of the most difficult medical cases: people with cancer, leukemia or HIV.

A few days later, my friend asked me to go with him and meet Lady Ana. I usually do not get very enthusiastic about meetings with spiritual Masters. I just let them happen without any expectations. However, before meeting her, a strong wave of energy passed through my body a couple of times. It was a sort of reconnection with my Self. I could feel much more centered and my mind stopped producing the many thoughts it used to.

Instinctively, I knew that I had inwardly asked for the meeting with Lady Ana and it had come to me in a natural way, because I was ready for it. I also knew that if the meeting was to take place, dramatic changes were about to happen in my life.

1991 WITH LADY ANA AFTER A GREAT MEDITATION TOGETHER

2012 WITH LADY ANA, A FEW WEEKS BEFORE SHE PASSED AWAY

No Mind State

I was waiting patiently on the bench sharing a fresh pretzel with some daring pigeons that were eating directly from my palm. I had arrived almost two hours before the meeting. One of my favorite pass-times involved sitting on a bench in nature, reading a book or feeding the birds. I did not even notice the old lady who had come to sit on the far end of the bench. I turned and when I looked into her eyes, I knew exactly who she was.

"I heard from your friend that you like to say 'my mind is silent when I meditate'. This is impossible," Lady Ana told me. "Figuratively, it might work, but literally the mind is absent of silence."

"So, there is no such thing as a silent mind?" I asked with great surprise.

"A silent mind does not exist. When silence comes, the mind disappears, vanishes and dissolves into nothing," she explained.

"It is as if saying that you are a living dead," she continued. "It makes absolutely no sense. If you are alive, then you are not dead. You cannot be both."

I looked at her. There was something there completely different compared to all the others I had met. In her early 60s, she had a remarkable and unique beauty coming from within. Your attention would be irresistibly drawn to the light in her eyes.

"They say that you are a great Master. They call you 'the great avatar of knowledge'," I said looking at her.

"You see? I was right. Your mind cannot stop. Close your eyes," Lady Ana told me. "See, sense and feel that you are just a wave in the vast ocean of the universe."

I complied immediately. A warm feeling gently opened my heart.

"How do you feel?" she asked.

"It is as if my center has left me and it has shifted to the center of the universe. I am not separate anymore. I am not afraid any longer," I answered.

"You see....this is the real you," Lady Ana commented with a smile. "You know how to fall back into unity with the universe; this unity gives you oneness. You feel blissful. All the conflicts and fears inside of you disappear and you feel refreshed and rejuvenated."

The Holistic Approach

I continued to work with Lady Ana for more than twenty years. Sometimes, I would fly from the other side of the world just to spend a couple of days near her.

Indeed, she was a great avatar of knowledge. She had a unique quality when it came to help, assist or heal somebody in need. She did not like the word "healing" much. She considered all humans as healed already, perfect beings, which is why she would use the word "correction of energies" more. She was able to connect instantly to the Akashic Records and "extract" the necessary information that one would need at that moment and in that place where they met her.

Like all other high level consciousness light beings that are here to guide us, Lady Ana knew exactly that, in order to help somebody, we need three things. First we need to ask permission to heal from the Higher Self of that person. Then, if we receive a positive response, we need to clean the karmic actions that we are all bound to, by diving deeply into their shallow waters. There, together with the person who has asked for assistance, we need to see the real cause of illness. And finally we need to mix all the information we have received and create a holistic approach that can really help the person who has asked for it.

The holistic approach used by Lady Ana was unique in the sense that she never used the same method to help everybody. Her hands performed magic. She knew exactly what meridian to press in order to release a blockage that had been keeping a person in pain for months.

One cannot imagine the energy that she was able to transfer from her hands to that specific point where the blockage was. It was as if you were touched by fire. Sometimes it would be intensely painful for a couple of moments and then, when the energy began to move correctly, you would feel newly born.

She would sometimes ask the person to repeat a specific word that related to the blockage in the body. The person would repeat that word or sentence for ten to fifteen minutes and feel a truly excruciating pain in a specific part of his or her body.

Lady Ana was a Master of clearing the emotional trauma connected to an illness. She knew exactly that an illness is caused either by an emotional trauma or by a belief pattern. I have only met one other person that has the capacity to do the same thing: that is Drunvalo Melchizedek.

Eventually, she would give a specific diet that would balance the masculine and feminine side in perfect harmony.

As a Mahavatar of knowledge, Lady Ana was able to use all the information related to the physical, emotional and mental body.

We had countless chats, sometimes for hours, sometimes for days, about I Ching, Upanishads, Bhagavad Gita, Brahmaputra, The Bible, The Quran, The Zohar, Torah and Tao Te Ching.

We extensively studied the work of Patanjali, Yoganada, Sri Yukteswar and the nine Buddhist devotional practices from Buddhanusmrti.

Needless to say, we had endless talks about Jesus, Buddha, Moses, Muhammad, Babaji, Lao-Tzu, Confucius, The Nagual Don Juan, St. Germain, Koot Hoomi, El Morya, Ramtha, Anastasia, Drunvalo Melchizedek and numerous other illustrious spiritual Masters that have, in one way or another, influenced spiritual life on this planet.

She contacted the Great White Brotherhood organization a few times and once, during an experiment where we used a specific aura reading apparatus, she invited an Ascended Master to join us. He referred to himself as Mark and allowed Lady Ana to record his specific aura. There is a clear difference between a multidimensional being and a human (see image of the Aura comparison on my website[1]).

Lady Ana used the holistic approach to help thousands of people from all over the world. Although she was born in the Republic of Moldova and she had spent most of her life in Romania, she would visit numerous other countries (including the US, Russia, Germany and France) where she held conferences and spiritual workshops with people from all over the world.

---

[1]www.danielmitel.com/wp-content/uploads/2016/03/Auras-comparisons.001.jpeg

Reconnecting with the Primordial Energy

The most important part of Lady Ana's work was what she used to call "the intuitive heart." Lady Ana's work was done in the most pure, feminine way. Her meditations and health-giving guidance were done on the spot; there was no prior planning, there were no schedules or manuals to be followed. It was a spontaneous guidance done in the moment, in the "now"; her intuition worked in perfect resonance with that instance.

Years of meditation together with her helped me grow and advance towards the feminine way of going into the heart.

Lady Ana liked to say that we need to move our "inner pilot" from the brain down to the heart; we need to "operate" from the heart not from the brain. Like all the other Masters who had achieved God's realization, she knew that operating from the heart was the most important step for a human being.

And like all Masters, the first thing she taught us was to connect with Mother Earth, Father Universe and the Higher Self. Her meditation was almost similar to the Tibetan meditations. She liked to call it "The Reconnection". She used to say that we must reconnect with the primordial energy, the ancient energy where we have come from.

As a matter of fact, it is indeed a reconnection. We have completely forgotten that our bodies were given to us by Mother Earth. We have completely forgotten that if we do not reconnect with Mother Earth's energy and Father Universe's vibration, we are not able to go into the heart. We have failed to remember that if we do not speak with our Higher Selves, then we are lost in our search for truth.

Let us review the main steps of the meditation[2].

First you need to find a place to stay for at least half an hour. Get into a comfortable posture, keeping your spine straight and your eyes closed. Place your attention on the top of your head and imagine that you are inhaling the word "relax" through the fontanel, your crown chakra.

Then see yourself somewhere in the middle of nature, a place that you know and love and become part of the earth; feel, for example, that you have become a tree with strong and powerful roots. Then see that you are literally the earth; all five elements of the Universe are inside you: earth, water, wood, fire and metal.

Feel that you are getting bigger and bigger and the whole Universe is around you. Orbit around the Sun. Feel the connection with the thousands of stars around you.

[2] The full mp3 audio file of this meditation (approx. 22 minutes) can be found on my website at www.danielmitel.com. You might be more comfortable if you run the audio file and close your eyes.

The Reversed Process

This spontaneous guidance of Lady Ana in her meditation was the essential part of our search in finding the secrets of our heart. All of us in the team working closely with her knew exactly that this step was a necessary key point in our spiritual evolution. Actually, it is the most important step in finding who we really are. Lady Ana knew that the only time we really are, is when we stop thinking. The moment we stop thinking, our inner guide enters.

Lady Ana used spontaneous guidance to bring us back to innocence. Spontaneous guidance, according to her enormous knowledge, is to be used to make us simple and innocent again. Because we are so involved in *doing*, we have almost completely forgotten about *being*.

We have forgotten that *being* is our real nature. *Doing* is just an accomplishment, a result of our daily activities. The Master had to help us become undivided again, free and able to move towards the heart.

The task was not easy because our minds could understand duality very easily and loved to cut the whole into pieces. We had this tendency to divide each thing that fell into our hands. Each book we read, each meditation we did, each exercise we carried out, had to be split and analyzed down to its lowest division. Lady Ana would smile as she watched our pathetic efforts and attempts to break apart and scrutinize everything about our existence.

We liked to chat for days and nights about all kinds of meditation techniques, about chakras and energies, auras and spiritual powers. She would listen patiently to all our talks and she would always join in the game like a little child.

She would laugh heartily and warmly at our assumptions about existence, the Infinite Universe and Divinity. She allowed our minds to turn towards the fragments, knowing perfectly well that the truth is a whole, not a piece.

Lady Ana helped us do a complete reversed process; she helped us synthesize and crystallize all the fragments from our minds. We would be in front of a giant puzzle and the Master would stand behind us gently helping us put each piece back in its place. We had to put back all these fragments and rebuild the whole that we had broken down earlier.

In order to go into our hearts, we needed to relearn the no-mind process. We needed to regain the trust in ourselves and we needed to have faith. She used some of the most powerful and simplest methods to bring us back to whom we really are: music, painting, connection with nature, and much more.

She would tell us to go out and listen to a Beethoven or Mozart concert in the middle of the day. On hundreds of mornings she would ask us to accompany her to the middle of the forest and relax near the spring water. There were many times when she would ask us to bring our paints and brushes and begin painting with our eyes closed.

Step by step, she dismantled our mental attitude of looking at things. It took us years to realize one simple thing: the divine or God, or whatever we named it, that hidden part that we were desperately seeking to find, was *here* and *now*.

The intuitive heart method was simple; when Lady Ana would see us in the no-mind attitude, she would work with us through a spontaneous guidance and bring us into the heart. It was so simple that when we arrived in the heart, it felt natural; it felt as if we were home again.

Entering the Heart
The Intuitive Way

I was very fortunate to use the intuitive method at the beginning of my quest. I was fortunate and blessed to be around the Master that brought my spirit back into my heart using the easiest, most uncomplicated and simplest method.

It was during one of our usual afternoon walks under the hundreds of linden trees on Copou Hill, the famous place where all the Universities of the city of Iași are situated. The fragrance of the linden tree flowers is one of a kind. We decided to stop and sit on the grass under an old linden tree. Heart-shaped leaves and fragrant blossoms in shades of yellow surrounded us.

We had come up the hill after a Bach concert. The heavenly music was still reverberating in our cells.

"Close your eyes," Lady Ana told us.

"See, sense and feel completely relaxed. Look at your mind and let it transform into a serene blue summer sky. It is as if you see it from below. All your thoughts are the white clouds moving across it."

We obeyed immediately. I noticed a calm and peaceful feeling.

"Let a gentle wind sweep all the white clouds towards the left until all of them have gone".

When the last cloud disappeared towards the left, an inner sound began to reverberate from the middle area of my chest.

"Feel or see where your heart is, or listen to the vibration that is coming from the middle of your chest. Listen to the sound of the heart and place your attention on it. It might be a vibration, a sound or the heartbeat," said Lady Ana.

In the beginning, I could clearly hear my heartbeat, the pulsation of the heart. Then the heartbeat began to fade and the vibration became stronger and stronger.

Intuitively, I followed the vibration and felt as if falling off a cliff. I almost became dizzy, but it was a very pleasant feeling. I was falling inside of me. I let it happen without resistance or anticipation. It was something irresistible that attracted me towards that direction, like a cosmic magnet.

Time and space became obsolete. I passed through thousands of stars and lights in just a few moments. Suddenly, I came to a stop. I did not stop in a compacted place It was a gentle end of the journey. I could see colors, waves of light and energy. I could sense the presence of other beings. I could move freely as if there was no gravitation.

Lady Ana was quiet. Surprisingly, I could see her there near me, in that place where my spirit had arrived. It was not just her, as a human appearance; it was much more. Rivers of lights and colors abundantly surrounded her. She was enormous in a beautiful way. I felt calm and detached; there was something protecting me.

I could see anything through just my intention. I could move to any place in the Universe through just my intention. I could create anything through just my intention. I could communicate anything to anybody, anywhere.

THE MASTER WITH FLOWERS. LADY ANA IN 2010

Chapter 6

The Indian Saints and Kriya of the Heart

The earliest time that I can recall in my life is when I was about three years old. I remember my mother watching me quietly as she would do her house chores. Her eyes would always express surprise as she watched me playing in silence, usually with a small pen and a piece of paper or with a small plastic basin that was a quarter of the size of a bucket. She would place the washed laundry in it and carry it outside to hang out in the sun.

Later, my mother would tell me that I used to be an unusually quiet child; I would never cry for food or water. She would caress me gently and pay attention more to my gestures and my eyes, than to the occasional words I would utter.

My favorite game was to sit on top of the small plastic basin with my legs crossed in a half lotus posture. Like a magnet, my tongue would be drawn to the roof my mouth above the soft palate and go into the nasopharynx, the well-known Kechari Mudra technique. I would feel a warm energy run up my spine and a sweet pleasant taste in my mouth. I would close my eyes and feel as if moving or flying through the void.

It took me a good many years to find out that I was actually practicing Kriya Yoga, the Spinal Breathing technique brought to humanity by Mahavatar Babaji. Practicing this technique was my first contact with Kundalini, the primary energy. This energy lays dormant in the base of the spine. Kriya Yoga, Spinal Breathing, is one of the best techniques to move the Kudalini up through the main energy centers of the spine.

Today, after many years of practicing and teaching Kriya Yoga, I have found together with my advanced students, that there is a very important stage of Kriya Yoga which is usually reached after a lot of Kriya Pranayama, Omkar and Thokar practice. Kriya Pranayama, the main technique of the First Kriya, enables the energy to move through the invisible subtle channels through which life energy flows inside the spinal column.

The main channels are Ida, the feminine energy or yin, flowing vertically along the left side of the spine and Pingala, the masculine energy or yang, flowing parallel to Ida on the right side of the spine. Right in the middle, is Sushumna, the principal channel that contains all the energy centers, the human chakras (see image on page 65).

The Omkar and Thokar techniques are part of the Higher Kriyas, empowering the heart chakra to function at its maximum capacity.

The Indian Saints, students of Mahavatar Babaji, would refer to the deep experience of the heart chakra activation as the foundation of all authentic spiritual paths. Lahiri Mahasaya, Sri Yukteswar, Yogananda and Satyananda would spend a substantial amount of time refining the energy of the heart.

KRIYA YOGA CHAKRAS

Entering the Heart
The Way of Prana

Many Kriya experts agree that the right combination of Kriya Pranayama, Omkar and Thokar practices, together with Japa (Contemplative Prayer), leads practitioners to the most important step in their spiritual journey: the movement of the spirit from the brain to the heart. I call it the Kriya of the Heart.

Japa or Contemplative Prayer is part of all spiritual schools. The Contemplative Prayer is the repetition of a sentence which has a devotional meaning. In Kriya, we use Lord Krishna's mantra "*Om Namo Bhagavate Vasudevaya*" as taught by Lahiri Mahasaya. The continuant use of this technique has the ability to bring devotees into the divine state of the Prayer of the Heart.

Simple concentration on breathing and on the practice of Kechari Mudra, combined with a mantra, can have a powerful effect on any practitioner. Kechari Mudra is a particularly important step. Ever since I was a child, I would keep my tongue in this position. Funnily enough, I was convinced that everyone around me kept their tongue in this position and was very surprised when a good friend from school told me that nobody can keep their tongue up for so many hours.

Kechari Mudra, which is part of ancient yoga traditions, can be practiced in different stages until the tongue can be effortlessly inserted into the nasopharynx, the upper part of the nasal cavity. In the beginning, we need to curl the tongue up and place the tip on the soft palate as far up as possible, until we are able to touch the uvula without straining the tongue.

There are different ancient texts that refer to the importance of Kechari Mudra. Buddha taught his disciples to press the tip of their tongue against the roof of their mouth, in order to control their thoughts and hunger. Various Hatha Yoga texts refer to Kechari Mudra power as a means to raise Kundalini, the primary energy, and access various reserves of Amrita, the divine liquid in the head, which subsequently floods the body. Personally, I can confirm the effect of this magical nectar: I spent a month in Tibetan caves and ten days in a retreat in Thailand where I sustained myself only on Amrita.

It is not my intention to initiate you to Kriya Yoga through this book, as this step takes the personal touch and supervision of a Kriya Master; however, I would like to share my experience of practicing the Kriya of the Heart.

Remember that, if we wish to achieve spiritual grace, we need to practice continuously; Lahiri Mahasaya's motto is "*Banat, Banat, ban jay!*" (Doing, doing, one day it is done!)

Some years of practice were sufficient to finally place my tongue in the Kechari Mudra, breathe rhythmically in Kriya Pranayama and begin a contemplative prayer.

After a while, my heart would start to vibrate continuously like a cosmic pulsar that emits regular light pulses. It is an inner calling that I cannot resist. It is like an interior magnet that attracts my undivided attention towards the heart. A warm feeling surrounds my chest and grows around my entire body like a protecting field of light.

I start moving inside my body like a spark of light inside the Universe. Sometimes it takes hours to cross space filled with galaxies and quasars, solar systems and stars into an infinite journey towards my heart.

Very often, I am still somewhere in the middle of the journey when I realize that three or four hours have passed and I need to get back into the day. I open my eyes and still feel a vibration in my whole body, especially in the area of the heart, for at least an hour or two.

Whenever I was able to cross time and space and arrive into the heart, I would feel born again. I would witness the great image of myself: pure, innocent and connected with Divinity.

Chapter 7

Mystics of Mount Athos, Saint Teresa of Avila and the Prayer of the Heart

One of the most rewarding times for any spiritual seeker are those spent doing the Prayer of the Heart. There are many groups of practitioners of the Prayer of the Heart, but I intend to speak about my experiences doing the techniques deriving from Mount Athos, St. Teresa of Avila and, in a later chapter, my experience with the Sufi dervishes.

If you decide to practice these techniques, initially you might think that there is a major difference between them and a different way of practicing and understanding the Prayer of the Heart, but eventually you will see the synergy between these methods and you will achieve the same end results. I can actually say that, when practiced wholeheartedly and in devotion, Kriya of the Heart can lead practitioners to the same results.

It is unfortunate that we have labeled the Masters who have achieved the unification with God with these methods, as Islamic Mystics, Orthodox Mystics or Catholic Mystics, thus destroying a sincere calling that comes to many spiritually oriented people. The Prayer of the Heart, its full achievement, lasts for a lifetime and continues beyond the physical lives of our bodies, regardless of the name or label we place upon it.

I am the best example, in that, regardless of the fact that I have practiced the Prayer of the Heart with Sufi Mystics up in the mountains of Iran, or with Orthodox Mystics of Mount Athos or with Indian saints of Kriya, they all welcomed and helped me in my quest for God realization.

It took me months and years before I was able to discover that the Prayer of the Heart happens in a very distinctive way; it arrives inside the mysterious and secret area of the heart. My breath and heart would stop for a short duration, and my eyes would fill with tears of inexpressible emotions.

Love for Beauty

The Greek book, "*Philokalia*" represents one of the most important collections of practical spiritual texts. Being part of the Eastern Orthodox hesychastic tradition and written between the fourth and fifteenth centuries, Philokalia provides us with the original guidance and instruction of the Orthodox Mystics in the practice of contemplative life. The title of the book is very suggestive: *Philokalia* means *Love for Beauty*. *Philia* means love and *Kallos* means beauty.

In the eighteenth century, two renowned Mystics, St. Nikodemos of the Holy Mountain and St. Makarios of Corinth, compiled the collection of texts into one single book that has become the principal spiritual text and guidance for many spiritual seekers all over the world. Philokalia is priceless: it represents the main workbook used by the Mystics of Mount Athos who practice hesychasm; there is no other written document of such great importance.

The book is enormous; the latest English version has five volumes. In other languages, in Romanian for example, Father Dumitru Staniloae had translated the entire original work in 1946, incorporating his own experience that has led to ten comprehensive volumes. There are also five volumes in the Russian language of more than a total of four thousand pages.

This book is a real treasure, full of advice and exercises; it is easy to read and understand, as the Mystics tried to explain it in an easy and effortless manner. As in all spiritual masterpieces, in Philokalia the Masters ask that we use our attention and intention continuously. The Mystics often call it "watchfulness" or "guarding our intellect"; sometimes they just call it attention and intention. Generally speaking, it is impossible to acquire any of the Mystics' virtues other than through watchfulness and observation of our own thoughts.

For those of you who intend to practice the Prayer of the Heart, you only need to pay close attention to certain parts of the book. Of course, feel free to read all the volumes, but particularly for the Prayer of the Heart, it is sufficient to read and practice certain exercises from this spiritual masterpiece. Therefore, you can read about the three kinds of prayer in part two of the book of Nikiphoros the Solitary, the book of Saint Gregory of Sinai (no need to read the short chapters) and of Simeon the New Theologian. These parts are essential for any practitioner of the Prayer of the Heart.

Also, if you have time, read the Discourse of Faith of Simeon the New Theologian and the book of Callistus and Ignatius. After some practice of the Prayer of the Heart, I recommend that you read the experience and guidance of all twenty-five Holy Fathers on the art of the true and essential prayer of the heart method. According to the instructions of the twenty-five Mystics, through the practice of constant prayer, our souls avoid any undesired and uncalled for acts and soon we are drawn to what is most essential: union with God.

The Masters ask that we continue practicing the prayer of the heart, placing emphasis on the importance and the necessity of the amount of time we spend praying.

I have witnessed the effect of constant prayer numerous times, especially in the monasteries from the north of Romania where the hesychastic Mystic monks pray without interruption.

The experience of the Russian pilgrim from the two books, *The Way of a Pilgrim* and *The Pilgrim Continues His Way* is also worth mentioning. The origin of these books still remains a mystery; the author is unknown and we do not know for certain whether it is literally a true story written by the narrator or whether it is a first person account of a particular pilgrim. According to some witnesses, there is a supposition that the author of the book is the Russian Orthodox monk, Archimandrite Mikhail Kozlov.

However, regardless of the origin and the intention of this anonymous author's fascinating story, the way in which his experience is narrated constitutes one of the best pieces of work in the field of spirituality. The pilgrim ideally represents a vast category of people who have spent their lives visiting monasteries in Mount Athos, in the Holy Land, seeking God through the Prayer of the Heart.

This pilgrim had found a spiritual teacher who had accepted him as a student and who gradually revealed to him the secret of Continuous Prayer. The pilgrim was instructed to repeat the Jesus Prayer 3000 times a day for two weeks, then 6000 times, then 12000 times. Eventually the pilgrim was able to literally breathe in and breathe out the prayer and experience the power of the divine light and the secret of the heart.

This pilgrim's life had completely changed; he quoted the Gospel passage of the birds of the air and the lilies of the field; he felt fully unified with and dependent on God. For those of us who practice the Prayer of the Heart, reading the pages of this book is like opening the infinite skies of the heart.

The Nine Virtues and the Eight Ruling Passions

One of the texts from Philokalia, written by St. Gregory of Sinai, suggests that those who practice hesychasm must work on the following five virtues:

1. silence
2. self-control
3. vigilance
4. humility
5. patience

The Mystic then mentions that there are three practices blessed by God:

1. psalmody (chanting)
2. prayer
3. reading

St. Gregory of Sinai added handiwork as one last virtue for those weak in the body. Obviously all nine virtues are essential for any spiritual practitioner of any method of enlightenment.

We have to understand that "those weak in the body" are those who cannot control their thoughts and their mind. This is an important topic that appears in different ways in almost each text of the book. St. Simeon the New Theologian clearly hints that if we do not guard our intellect, we cannot attain purity of the heart. It is overall impossible to achieve any of these nine virtues in any way other than through watchfulness. Therefore, basically, we need to apply attention and intention.

The Master continues his advice by asking that we work hard on achieving three things: the **first** is to respect everything that comes to us, regardless if it is reasonable or senseless. The **second** is to try to achieve a pure conscience, through actions of kindness. The **third** is to be completely detached, with our thoughts inclined towards nothing worldly; we should basically avoid any conflict or competition, so as to allow our ego to slowly disappear.

On the same topic, another famous Mystic, Evagrios the Solitary, asks that we be continuously alert and protect ourselves from our thoughts as we do the Prayer of the Heart. Then we can complete our prayer and continue our activities in stillness and peace. The Master explains that we cannot carry out a pure prayer if we are caught in material things and agitated by constant cares.

Another important topic written by St. Gregory of Sinai is on the *eight ruling passions*: **gluttony**, **avarice** and **self-esteem** - the three principal passions; **unchastity**, **anger**, **dejection**, **listlessness** and **arrogance** - the *five subordinate passions*.

The Master asks that we develop specific behaviors that change the eight ruling passions:

1. generosity
2. self-control
3. humility
4. purity

5. gentleness
6. joy
7. courage
8. self-belittlement

Combined with **faith, patience, love** and the **nine virtues**, these specific behaviors are highly helpful and bring us all the more closer to our divine state.

As for food, all the Mystics have given the same advice: a pound of bread is enough for anyone aspiring to attain a state of inner silence. Furthermore, they say that our food should consist of whatever is at hand, not what we crave for. The best and the shortest guiding rule for spiritual seekers is to maintain a good mix of fasting, vigilance and prayer of the heart.

Entering the Heart
The Method of Simeon, the New Theologian

When practicing entering the heart with the Prayer of the Heart method, I extensively apply the method of Simeon the New Theologian. These instructions are clear and straightforward. Faith and patience are the main qualities required during this exercise. We must remember Master Lahiri Mahasaya's motto *"Banat, Banat, ban jay!"* (Doing, doing, one day it is done!)

I will first describe this method and then I will share my experience of doing it.

First we need to find a quiet place, a place where we meditate pray or do spiritual exercises. It is good to be in the same place every time because we charge it with a specific vibration that always helps us connect with our inner self faster.

Then we need to stop our thoughts. Simeon the New Theologian says that we need to withdraw our intellect from everything worthless.

The next step is to rest our chin on our chest and focus our gaze on the center of our belly or on our navel. Our attention must be fully concentrated on gazing at the center of our belly or our navel with no thoughts wondering around.

Then we need to calm down our breathing; we need to breathe really slowly and gently.

As we continue to practice gazing and breathing, we close our eyes and start to search for the place of our heart within us, where the Mystic says that all the powers of the soul reside.

In the beginning we will find darkness there and an impenetrable density. Later, as we continue to practice day and night, we will miraculously find an unceasing joy.

As soon as we find the place of the heart, the Master says that we will see things which we had been previously unaware of. We will see an open space within the heart that is entirely luminous and full of discernment.

From this moment on, any distractive thoughts that may appear, will be driven away and immediately destroyed before they come into full fruition.

Simeon the New Theologian says that we will learn the rest ourselves, with the help of God, by keeping guard over our mind and retaining Jesus in our heart. As the saying goes, *"Stay in your meditation room and it will teach you everything."*

When I practice this method, I try to use the same place although it is somewhat difficult for me on account of my extensive travel program all over the world. However, even when I am in a training room alone or in my hotel room on the other side of the world, I can still practice it very easily.

I always start with some stretching exercises, as keeping the chin on the chest for a long time is particularly difficult. The neck and the spine need to be warmed up before starting this practice. I usually exercise Maha Mudra which is a very simple and rewarding Kriya Yoga technique.

Then I find a comfortable position, usually in the half lotus posture, with which I can keep my spine straight, but also rest my chin on the chest. I start gazing at my navel for a couple of minutes and then I start breathing slower and slower. I allow my mind to quieten. My inhalation and exhalation are so gentle, that I almost cannot see any movement of the abdomen area.

Usually within ten or fifteen minutes, my breathing almost disappears and then I close my eyes gently and try to find the place of the heart. This step is not as difficult as it seems, because one of the effects of the previous step (breathing-in and breathing-out gently) is the awareness of the heartbeat. I can really feel the heartbeat; the pulsation of the heart gets stronger and stronger and, therefore, it becomes easier for me to find the place of the heart.

Another thing that happens when I feel the heartbeat is an inner vibration, similar to the sound that a bee makes, coming from the area of the heart.

After I find the heart and place my attention on it, I can see an open space within the heart that is filled with a powerful light. I cannot distinguish a specific source from where this light comes from, as it appears from all directions. Indeed from this point on, all the distractive thoughts disappear completely and a divine peace permeates my entire being.

Entering the Heart
the Method of Nikiphoros the Monk

Another way to go into the heart is given by Nikiphoros the Monk. This Mystic uses two ways: the Breathing method, a technique that is also largely used by Tibetan and Himalayan Masters and the Heart Concentration Method.

First, let me explain the **Breathing Method** and then I will share my experience of this procedure. Nikiphoros strongly suggests we find a Master or a Teacher that can guide us on the spiritual path so that we can arrive into the heart easier. He asks us to diligently and continuously search for a guide and if we do not find one then we must renounce our worldly attachments, call on God and start practicing alone.

As in the previous method, first we need to find a quiet place, a place where we meditate, pray and do our spiritual exercises. Again, it is good to be the in same place every time, because we charge that place with a specific vibration that always helps us in our practice.

Then, we need to concentrate our mind and lead it into the respiratory passage through which our breath passes into our heart.

We need to apply more pressure on our mind and compel it to descend with our inhaled breath into our heart. The Mystic says that, once the mind has entered there, it becomes united with the soul and fills with indescribable delight.

We need to train our mind not to leave the heart quickly, because, at first, it is strongly disinclined to remain constrained in this way. But once it gets used to staying there, it can no longer bear to be outside the heart.

Then all external things become irrelevant and peripheral. If, after the first attempts, we have managed to enter through our mind into the heart, we need to give thanks to God and continually persevere in this practice.

I really enjoy practicing this method. Before Nikiphoros, Buddha had used this method with his disciples. It is still used by Tibetan and Himalayan Masters. Buddha advised his students to practice it anytime during the day, but especially before falling asleep. It helps to dream from the heart and dreams become clean and uncontaminated by negative thoughts.

I like to practice this method in a quiet place; in the middle of nature whenever possible. Nevertheless, it can be practiced anywhere; sometimes I even practice during my flights while travelling and it works very well.

In the beginning, for a couple of minutes I try to feel my breathing pattern without changing it. I might breathe deeper or shallower and my breathing might even pause for a couple of moments. I just observe it without any intervention.

Then I try to let my mind follow the breathing flow, just as a leaf follows a waterfall. Sometimes, it is tricky because my mind tries to move away and escape the breathing flow. Indeed, as the Mystics have said, being watchful and vigilant, applying our attention and intention, is the key to success on the spiritual path.

After I have descended into my heart with my inhaled breath, I feel an inexpressible happiness and joy. My mind and my soul are unified and I am filled with peace and harmony.

I need to keep focus on my mind so that it does not leave the heart quickly, as, during this exercise, the mind has a tendency to leave the heart and move back into the brain.

Then all external things become irrelevant and I am completely detached and in peace. I always say a prayer and give thanks to God.

The second way to go into the heart given by the Byzantine Mystic, Nikiphoros the Monk, is the **Heart Concentration Method**.

The Master asks that we use this method if, after having tried the breathing method as much as possible, we are still not able to enter the realms of the heart.

First we need to banish our thoughts and completely quieten our mind. Then we focus on the chest area, on the location of the heart and we start to repeat the prayer of Jesus ceaselessly: "*Lord Jesus Christ, Son of God, have mercy on me*".

If we continue focusing on the heart and continuously repeat this prayer then, after some time, our heart will open and we will be able to easily use the first method, the breathing technique, so that we may enter the heart.

That is when, as Nikiphoros tells us, the whole choir of virtues - love, joy, peace and the others - will come to us.

I find this method very easy and pleasant to practice and the first time I practiced it, my mind had become completely quiet without any thoughts after just a few days.

This method is widely applied in India and in Tibet with the use of different prayers or mantras. The Great Kriya Master, Lahiri Mahasaya, would use this method and change the prayer according to the group of students he was teaching it to. Therefore, in one group of students he would use the Vasudeva Mantra, "*Om Namo Bhagavate Vasudevaya*", while for another group he would use "*Lâ Ilâha Illâ Allâh*". I often use the Tibetan Prayer of love and peace: "*I Am Pure Love And Bliss; I am in Light and Peace*".

Practicing these methods helps me understand that there is a huge difference between praying with the mind in the head and praying with the mind in the heart. In a chapter further below, I explain how modern science has already demonstrated that the heart has a large group of brain cells that gives the heart the capacity to make decisions over the brain. Basically we have a brain in the heart!

Personally, as I did these exercises, it had become even more important for me to discover that there is a forever now, an everlasting presence. My whole attention had reached such cohesion that nothing externally was able to distract me.

Entering the Heart
Nine Stages by St. Teresa of Avila

One of the most important works related to the Prayer of the Heart has been given to us by the prominent Spanish Mystic, St. Teresa of Avila. A reformer of the Carmelite Order, she is considered to be one of the most well known theologians of contemplative prayer. Her teachings originate from her own experience and complete the hesychastic tradition.

Although I did not use this method exactly in the order described by the Spanish Mystic in her teachings, I was often brought to similar experiences during my meditation, or my time of chanting and prayer.

This Master explains that there are nine stages of prayer, not nine different techniques as some practitioners are inclined to believe. Once we start the contemplative prayer we experience each stage as we arrive at that level of consciousness.

While using different methods of meditation, I was able to go into the heart in a natural way and, later, I could identify a specific stage from this Mystic's teachings.

These stages are:

1. Vocal Prayer
2. Meditation
3. Affective Prayer

4. Active Recollection
5. Infused Recollection
6. Prayer of the Quiet
7. Prayer of the Union
8. Prayer of Conforming Union (Ecstatic Union)
9. Prayer of Transforming Union

Below is a brief description of each stage, so that we may better understand how they can help us connect with our heart.

Vocal Prayer: St. Teresa of Avila recommends this stage for beginners of this practice. We choose the mantra or prayer that triggers in us much devotion and passion and we start repeating it. As the Spanish Mystic tells us, this is the door through which we enter the "inner castle."

Meditation: After some time of preliminary vocal prayer, there is a stage in which we fight against distractions and disturbances. During this stage, we sometimes need to stop for a couple of moments and resume the mantra or prayer, until we find peace and peacefulness.

Affective Prayer: This is the stage where we find our hearts; we feel peace and kindness within. We can see, sense and feel inner light and inner vibration.

Active Recollection: This is the stage in which the prayer or mantra continues naturally; we feel as if in a trance and everything around us seems like a dream.

Infused Recollection: Here, we start to really feel the presence of God within us and around us; it is the stage where we feel divine grace entering our heart.

Prayer of the Quiet: This is the first stage of advanced prayer. Our memories slowly fade and we feel the intimate awareness of God permeating our soul and body. It is also referred to as the first stage of mystical prayer.

Prayer of the Union: Here, all our inner faculties are occupied by God; our memory and imagination are completely captivated by divine grace. The intensity of this mystical experience is beyond words.

Prayer of Conforming Union (Ecstatic Union): The last two stages, the ecstatic union and transforming union, are the last two degrees of mystical prayer. In ecstatic union, we feel as if we are on an ecstatic flight; sometimes, our body is literally lifted into space. Sometimes the soul goes out by itself; the experience is so profound that one never wants it to end.

Prayer of Transforming Union: Many Mystics identify this last stage of mystical prayer with "mystical marriage." It is the highest degree of perfection that one can attain in this life. It is a total transformation of the soul into the One. Divine love is totally expressed to us. The Mystics say that the Trinity, The Universal Father, Eternal Son and Infinite Spirit (The Mother), are fully experienced by our soul.

From the third stage up to the last one, the heart prevails. I was able to feel the presence of God inside me. The "recollection" is actually the remembrance of who I really am.

There are two different types of recollection and the Spanish Mystic attempts to give us a hint about each one. In the fourth stage, the active recollection, I almost felt numb, as if in a trance.

Then, in the fifth stage, I was "infused" with divine grace, the infused recollection.

Words cannot describe the last four stages. These are mystical stages in which sometimes, for a couple of moments, I would have a hint of what "mystical marriage" means, the union with the Divine. In these stages, I also felt a powerful, but ecstatic pain, within me. Sometimes I would be unconscious, almost fainting; sometimes I would remain without breathing for minutes.

My eyes would fill with tears and the experience was so intense that I almost felt as if an arrow had penetrated my heart. The pain would be sweet, but powerful; I would avoid eating, so as to prevent the experience from ending. I could stay in that stage all my life, just enjoying the divine grace in my soul.

Chapter 8

The Heart Imagery Masters

In my previous books, *This Now Is Eternity* and *Heart Imagery: A Path To Enlightenment*, I have written extensively about my experiences with the two Heart Imagery Masters, Karma Dorje and Tenzin Dhargey. Both books contain valuable information about the history of Heart Imagery, starting from the Adamic Race until the present time. The books include a precious amount of exercises and meditations that can be practiced by anyone who does not have any prior spiritual experience.

The Heart Imagery Masters, Karma Dorje and Tenzin Dhargey, compared us to circles without centers. They used to say that people in the world are superficial. When we are in the center of the circle we are balanced. We are "*kunchen*": all knowing. But people in the world live only on the circumference of the circle. They talk and talk and talk and their words do not carry any authentic meaning, because they are not centered. Their whole consciousness consists of the outside world. They are without, not within. Their words are without meaning. Their minds are constantly working. Their minds never stop. Not even when they sleep. When they sleep, they dream of others; they think of others even when they sleep. When they are alone, in their mind they are still surrounded by hundreds of people and they are in the middle of a crowd. When they talk, their words may be understood, but they do not carry any meaning.

The Masters used to tell me that we are in the center is only when we are in very deep sleep; when we do not dream at all. But then again, we are totally unconscious. So, basically, we are conscious only when we are on the circumference of the circle. That means, however, that we are rarely centered. And even when we are centered, we are not conscious. It is like the living dead. Life can never be known on the circumference. Life can only be known in the center, at the core, when we are in the heart.

Entering the Heart
the Heart Imagery Method

One of the easier methods to go into the heart is the Heart Imagery Method. Prior to any imagery exercises, Masters Karma Dorje and Tenzin Dhargey would give me a simple exercise to move me from the brain to the heart. They would tell me that this method is naturally experienced, especially by children.

Let's summarize this technique.

First find a comfortable position, keeping your spine straight and close your eyes.

Breathe out three times: draw in a normal breath and let out a long, slow exhalation through the mouth; as you exhale, see all your problems, issues, concerns and internal conflicts moving out and away. Then breathe in and out normally.

Now see, sense and feel that you are a big house. Imagine a room on top of the house; it is the room of the brain. A spiral staircase descends from the middle of this room (and the middle of your brain) to the middle of your chest.

Use your intention and go down the stairs.

When you arrive at the middle of your chest, step off the stairs and slowly turn to your left.

There is a door there that goes into your heart. It can be any type of door you imagine.

Open the door and step inside your heart; remember to close the door behind you.

Now see, sense and feel the power and love emanating from your heart.

If you read this method three-four times and then try to do it, you will be surprised at how easy it is to go into the heart.

I have few recommendations especially for the first time you practice this. First, once you are in the heart, you will see images, places, worlds and faces of known and unknown people. To be sure that you are actually in the heart and that it is not just your imagination, verify whether the light inside of the heart is polarized or non-polarized.

This is a very simple step. When the light is polarized, as it is in the brain, we can clearly see the shadows of the objects or the persons. This is because there is a source of light, which is the sun. Therefore, shadows are always caused by its light. However, the light in the heart is not polarized and there are no shadows.

I find that this is the simplest method to go into the heart. Even if you do not manage to go into the heart on your first attempt, by continuing to practice, especially in combination with heart imagery exercises, you will soon be able to experience love and harmony deriving from your heart. During the Heart Imagery workshops, hundreds of people from all over the world have revealed how they have experienced and felt their heart.

One of the most common revelations is that there is a whole universe inside our hearts.

It is amazing to see how easy and beautiful it is to live from the heart.

Chapter 9

The Sacred Flame of Love

Almost thirty years ago I had the rare opportunity to connect with one of the most ancient civilizations of this planet while looking for a place where the last headquarters of the Adamic Race used to be. It is on the mountain range of Kopet Dagh that extends over 500 km within Turkmenistan and Iran. My aim was to visit the highest Iranian summit, Mount Quchan (3191 meters), which I understood from the Tibetan Masters to be literally the last place where the Adamic Race had lived before splitting up towards different directions with the purpose of helping humanity raise its level of consciousness.

After Kopet Dagh, I eventually ended up on the opposite side of Iran, in some villages up in the mountains of the Zanjan area, east of Tehran. The houses there were virtually embedded inside the mountain. When I arrived, I had the feeling that I had travelled through time; I was invited to participate in an ancient Zoroastrian ritual that made me feel as if I were in a world that had lived over 2500 years ago.

People from these villages still have the fire of Zoroaster burning day and night. I asked them why they use fire in their meditation and prayer rituals and they explained that it actually represents the dual light that comes from the sun and the unity light that can be found inside our heart.

Before entering the sanctuary of Zoroaster, I washed myself with pure, crystal clear spring water; it is a requirement for those entering the sanctuary to purify themselves with water. In the middle of this place was the holy fire. I joined the circle of people who were gazing at the fire burning continuously for over 2500 years.

As I watched the fire, I felt the presence of Zoroaster, the prophet and Master that conceived those values we still hold sacred to this day. Long before other Masters, it was Zoroaster who had taught us about the Supreme Being. The fire that has been burning day and night for centuries in fact represents a flame of love for life.

The Mystic's Dance of the Heart

The most important moment of my visit was when I was invited to join the ecstatic dance of *Sama* with Sufi dervishes as an initiation in this ancient method. I had heard a lot of stories about this mystical dance and about the dervishes that belong to the secret Mevlevi Order, so I happily accepted to participate in the ritual. Their secret meetings take place in centers known as *hanavah*; many are still shut down by local authorities every day.

The place was filled with men of different ages. I knew that they were Sufi dervishes and that the ritual I was allowed to participate in was for men only. However, I was told that women have similar rituals in which men are not allowed to participate.

My friend told me that the dancing dervishes believe in the existence of two worlds: the physical or the seen world and the virtual or the unseen world. He explained that this dance would help me shift easily from one world to another. The dervishes believe that, in order to enter the unseen world, we need to arrive to the stage of enlightenment from where we can hear the voice of God.

The Sama dance, *Sama* meaning "to hear", helps dervishes achieve a state of ecstasy, the "*wajd*" as Sufi Masters call it, which literally means to find. So by listening to the music and dancing to the rhythm of the dervishes, one can find the divinity within themselves.

In the center of the large circular room was the Master; an elderly man with a long white beard. We bowed down to him in respect and then formed a large circle around him. After a long period of meditation, we stood up and formed another large circle. The music started softly in the background; a group of men chanted, while some of them skillfully played hand drums.

In one corner of the room stood the Chief Sama Dancer and we passed in front of him three times, each time exchanging greetings until we had formed the circling movement. We had to perform the dance on our right foot with accelerating speed. Our arms clasped together, we moved continuously in a circular movement as the music became louder and the rhythm faster. As we continued to dance, our head was tilted and only the upper body was moving. As the dervishes danced, their long hair swayed back and forth like in a dream.

We danced continuously for more than an hour. Some of dervishes were moving so gently that I thought they were levitating. Later, my friend confirmed to me that this was not just an impression.

As the beat of the drums sped up, we entered into a trance. Some of us went into a meditative state, some were levitating and some continued to dance, swirling around. We were in this state of ecstasy, the "*wajd*", as the Sufi Masters call it. I went to a corner and closed my eyes, entering into meditation. During this dance, I had instantly entered my heart, so I continued the magical journey into the infinite.

As Rumi, the founder of the Mevlevi Order, says, we are all a speck of light in the universe. For Rumi, Sama is the nourishment of the soul. He says that the Sama dancing dervishes represent the solar system and the planets that revolve around the sun. Even as they revolve around the sun, they are also immersed in their own microcosm, creating new worlds and making contact with the infinite spirit.

Indeed, while on the surface it seemed that we were performing this choreography of the cosmos, dancing to its rhythm, at the same time we were in inner contact with an ancient awareness that humanity has forgotten. Our feet may have been touching the earth, but our souls were merging with the cosmos. According to the Mevlevi philosophy, with this dance dervishes understand the possibility of the eternity of the soul, because while the body is still touching the earth, the mind and soul breaks free from the bondage of earth.

I have heard about a theory that interprets the ritual dance as a way in which to unite with the cosmic powers and eternity. The same theory says that the rotation of the dance is related to three different movements within the human body. The first regards the movement of the electrons; the other has to do with the movement of the molecules and the third with the movement of the cells. Accordingly, the electrons are related to emotions, the molecules to the intelligence or the mind, and the cells to physicality and thus to the earth.

As I performed the Sama dance, I could see, sense and feel
that there are three movements inside our body that occur
simultaneously. These movements have different effects on each
practitioner. Later, after the dance, I had the opportunity to ask
the dervishes about these movements and they all confirmed
them. All of us had experienced them, not just me.

First I could sense that the constant movement of the body
produces a movement of the cells inside the body; the velocity
of the dance creates an internal harmony that produces a high
level of consciousness. At the same time, the movement of the
head activates the pineal gland and eventually the pineal
chakra in the middle of the brain. Subsequently, my third eye
was instantly activated. Finally, after ten or fifteen minutes
of dancing, the dormant Kundalini at the base of the spine
began to awaken. I felt as if ants were crawling up my spine;
a sweet and tingling sensation associated with a sound like the
snapping of a whip.

When all these three inner movements happen
simultaneously, the spirit moves into the heart in a natural
movement. It took me less than ten minutes to feel the effect
of all three movements and enter the heart.

Chapter 10

The Chakra of Unconditional Love

There is another way to go into the heart that the Tibetan Masters, Karma Dorje and Tenzin Dhargey, applied very often. They told me that this way works very well especially for practitioners who know and use the main human energy centers: the chakras. They call it the *Way of Pure Love* because it is related with the chakra of the heart that is responsible for unconditional love.

Karma Dorje and Tenzin Dhargey explained that we have two main heart chakras (see image on page 101). The first one, the chakra of unconditional love is situated in the middle of the body inside the prana tube at the level of the inferior end of the sternum bone (the xiphoid process small bone). The second chakra is located in the middle of the chest and the Masters call it the Chakra of Emotions.

Both chakras play a major role within the energy of the human bodies. The Chakra of Emotions needs to be harmonized every time we have an emotional issue, a conflict or a disagreement that changes our energy and makes us stressed and angry. It is the seat of emotional traumas and we need to clean it continuously until all the intense emotions are gone.

According to the Tibetan Masters, if we do not use a method to clean the Chakra of Emotions, sooner or later we fall ill and our physical body suffers greatly.

I strongly advise spiritual seekers to clean their emotional traumas before starting their inner journey in search of divine grace and remembering who they really are. There are different methods to do it; the simplest ones are healing through Rebirthing techniques and the exercises from Heart Imagery workshops.

An important role is played by the three spheres (see image on page 101) of energy that surround the navel chakra, the chakra of unconditional love and the pineal chakra in the middle of the brain. These spheres are literally reserves of energy connected with the prana tube that crosses through the middle of our body.

There are different ways to bring prana in these three spheres. The usual way of bringing energy in the lower sphere, the navel sphere, is with the ancient Chinese exercises of Qi Gong or Tai Chi that fortify and strengthen the energy in the body.

The easiest way to bring energy in the middle sphere is through the prana tube; breathe in prana until you see, sense and feel that the sphere is filled with life force energy.

The upper sphere, or the halo, is activated when the third eye is activated. There are different ways to activate the third eye, but I always advise my students to do it after their spirit has moved into the heart.

THE THREE SPHERES OF ENERGY, THE PRANA TUBE, THE MERKABA AND THE LEONARDO SPHERE

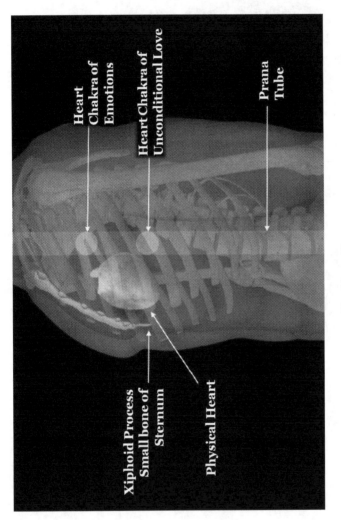

The Heart Chakras

Entering the Heart
the Natural Way of the Heart Chakra

The intuitive way of the Heart Chakra begins, as mentioned in the previous chapter, with an intense clearing of emotional traumas and deeply distressing or disturbing experiences that have taken place in our lives. All the Masters I was blessed to meet and work with until now have said the same thing: the best way to clear these experiences is to forgive all the people with whom we have been in the conflict or disagreement.

It might be difficult and sometimes exhausting, but forgiving these people with whom we have been in friction clears all the survival negative emotions that keep our minds distracted by unnecessary energy-consuming thoughts.

When we feel that we have cleared the path and we have forgiven all the people with whom we have had a dispute or who have made us suffer, then we are ready to go into the heart using the intuitive way of the Heart Chakra of Unconditional Love.

The steps are easy to follow once we feel free of negative thoughts.

Basically we first need to move from the middle of the brain, where the Pineal Chakra is located, down to the Throat Chakra, at the base of the throat; then to the second Heart Chakra, that is located in the middle of the chest (the Chakra of Emotions) and finally down to the Heart Chakra of Unconditional Love.

From there we need to let our inner self or higher self guide us towards the heart. The physical heart is situated slightly to the left, in front of the Chakra. Therefore, we need to allow our attention to go in that direction. We also place a strong intention behind the attention and soon we arrive into the heart. Sometimes it takes many attempts to enter the heart, but after we have become accustomed to this method, it becomes really easy and natural to use it.

Chapter 11

The Wisdom of the Native People

They say we are their "younger brothers and sisters" and they are right. We call them the native or the aboriginal people who still preserve the wisdom of their ancestors throughout the millenniums without having altered it. They do not need prescriptions and pills to be healthy; they do not need watches to tell the time. They do not need a weather report to know that rainfalls or storms are coming. They know the alignment of the planets exactly and the retrogrades of each celestial body in our solar system without the use of a telescope or an artificial satellite. They still use the most accurate and precise calendar.

They are still here, living in peace and harmony with Mother Earth. Especially in the Americas, Australia and New Zealand, the native people try to keep the values of this planet intact. These values are respect for animals and nature and living in harmony with the universe. The Kogi in Columbia, the Mayans in Yucatan, the Waitaha in New Zealand, the Hopi in Arizona, Tibetans in the Himalayas and the list goes on, are the people whose ancestors lived in the old continent of Lemuria and who had spread all over the world.

Their wisdom and knowledge is invaluable and essential to keep the balance of the unharmonized way of living of the rest of us. Unfortunately, the majority of them went quietly into the forests, jungles and mountains when they saw the level of destruction we are causing Mother Earth and implicitly to ourselves. However, they have not given up on us. They love us because we are literally their younger brothers and sisters.

I have had numerous meetings with different native cultures that showed me crucial information about the way we should live in order to balance ourselves and be in harmony with Mother Earth. All native cultures speak of Mother Earth, Father Universe. Some native cultures speak of our Father Sun or Father Galactic Sun and our Higher Selves. Some speak of our Inner Selves or Inner Guides.

The natives explain that, though we have biological parents, we also have cosmic parents or divine parents. According to their knowledge, our divine parents are Divine Mother Earth, Divine Father Universe and our Divine Higher Selves.

In numerous cultures, the representation of the Divine Father Universe is directly related to the sun. Some cultures relate the Divine Father Universe to the Unity Consciousness Grid that surrounds our planet, which has a vital role in protecting us against cosmic radiations, solar flares and coronial mass ejections that the sun periodically releases into the solar system.

Large native cultures, such as the Mayans, still use accurate cosmic calendars that give them a lot of information about the behavior of the sun and the surrounding celestial planets or cosmic bodies.

In December 2012, I was part of a group that connected with Mayan Elders in Mexico. We were visiting the pyramids in Yucatan and we had the amazing opportunity to meet some of the wisest people living in the remote areas of Mexico.

I was surprised to see the great interest of the Mayans in our education and our enlightenment. I spoke with Don Pedro Pablo Chuc, the Mayan Elder, and he showed me a school where the Mayans invite people from all over the world to learn their wisdom and knowledge.

Situated in a remote village in Yucatan, the teachers of this school are some of the best Mayan Elders who have decided to share all their knowledge with us starting with Mother Earth, understanding and awareness and also about the cosmic cycles of the universe and our solar system. To learn more about the project, offer assistance and become part of it, please contact me and I will provide you with the details.

It is outstanding to see how native people all over the world are taking the initiative to help us reconnect with nature and the universe.

Don Pedro Pablo Chuc Pech, Head of Itza Mayan Council of
Elders, and Daniel Mitel
December 21, 2012 in Yucatan, Mayan Land, Mexico

Entering the Heart
the Heart of the Earth Method

Never in the history of humanity has there been a more important time to reconnect with Mother Earth than now. Native people are warning us that if we do not do this now, it may be too late for humanity. It is hard to say what "too late" may mean. The natives themselves do not know with precise accuracy about the events that might happen within the next couple of years, but they feel and sense that we are completely unbalanced and that we need to reconnect with our planet.

Native people actually do not practice any exercise or ritual, meditation or spiritual activity without first connecting to Mother Earth. Some of them, such as the Kogi Mamas from Columbia, address us from their location in the middle of nature and they are often barefooted, grounding themselves during their talk.

All aboriginal people know an ancient secret: if we connect with the heart of the earth, then we can enter our own heart in a natural way. They say that this is very easy to do.

The first step is to find a place in the middle of nature where you can relax, close your eyes and breathe rhythmically; a quiet place where you can hear the songs of birds and feel the breeze gently touching your skin. You might hear the sound of the spring water gently running into the valley or the sounds of waves touching the shore; any place where you feel relaxed and enjoy nature around you.

You might even be barefoot with your feet gently touching the ground or the grass. While you relax, keep your eyes closed and try to feel your heart in the middle of your chest. Slow down your breathing and listen to the heartbeat.

Feel your love for this place, for Mother Earth. Allow this love to grow inside of you. Then see, sense and feel a beam of light going down from your heart to the heart of Mother Earth, to the center of the earth. Allow all your love to go down through this beam of light towards the heart of Mother Earth. Feel and literally see waves of love and light travelling from your heart towards the heart of Mother Earth.

Place all your attention and intention on this process and soon you will feel Mother Earth's response. It is like a warm cloud of light coming from below, entering first through your feet, then continuing up, penetrating each and every atom of your body.

This energy calms down all your thoughts and memories. You feel protected and safe from any danger. Your cosmic Mother helps and protects you. This powerful vibration might remain with you for hours, even for days if you love to be in nature or if you have activities in nature.

Chapter 12

The Yogi of the Himalayas

The outskirts of Kathmandu Valley are some of the most beautiful images to be found on our beloved Mother Earth. I have passed through Dhulikhel, the small Nepalese village located on the Eastern rim of Kathmandu Valley, south of the Himalayas admiring the unearthly and mysterious places that are surrounding this famous area.

Swami Vivekananda and Paramahansa Yoganada are just some of the illustrious Masters that had passed through this area in their quest to meet the Mystic yogi of the Himalayas.

Having come from Tibet's border town of Kodari, I was passing through this area going towards the Ugratara Janagal village in the Bagamati zone of central Nepal when, after some strange and inexplicable situations, I connected with a group of local Brahmins, Dalits and Tamangs who are the local people in that area.

What happened was mysterious and baffling. The bus came to a stop right in the middle of the village and did not move anymore. It was as if an invisible hand had stopped the engine right in the middle of the dusty road. The driver got out and was staring at the engine completely puzzled.

In a confused state of being, he said over and over again, "Nothing is wrong with the engine! Why does it not work? Why does it not work?" In the end, he told us that he needed to call a mechanic to check the engine. We all got our bags out and began wandering around, trying to find another way to reach the Ugratara Janagal village.

The powerful sun was burning hot, so I looked around for a place to buy some water from. I stopped at a small kiosk in the middle of the village and took out some rupee coins. An old Brahmin was sitting in a lotus posture near the kiosk, reciting invocations and litanies from the ancient Rigveda. He gave me a long look and asked me in perfect English: "Why are you spending the coins for water that is not alive?"

I looked in the eyes of the old man and felt a strange energy crossing through the center of my forehead.

"There is a group of Brahmins, Dalits and Tamangs passing through in few moments. Why not join them and go towards the water of life?" the old Brahmin suggested smiling and looking at me with his big eyes. His eyes were shining as if they carried in them two powerful lights.

Indeed, a few moments later, a group of people passed by us. The old man encouraged me to go with them. Without asking or explaining, I joined the group and followed them on their road. No one said anything; it was as if I had always been a part of the group.

Funnily enough, as soon as we began to move, I could hear the bus start its engine from a distance; I knew that it was too late to catch it, but I did not care anyway. I turned my head once more towards the old man who was still watching me as we moved away; he slightly bowed his head towards me as a sign of support and trust. I could feel his love for me as if he was a parent or an elderly brother. Deep inside my heart, I knew that he and I had been on the same path a long time ago.

The Holy Water of the Dhulikhel Himalayans

We were walking for more than an hour on a path in the magnificent mountain when, suddenly, the man in front stopped and came towards me. He told me in a very gentle tone that my road had ended there. Indeed, I could see spring water on the right side of the path flowing down to the valley.

I thanked him from all my heart for guiding me to this place and he smiled back telling me that they were honored to bring me there. Then, while the group began to depart, he turned his head once more and said: "They are expecting you."

I did not understand what he meant by that, but by then I had become so accustomed to situations like this one, that I had stopped asking. I had learned to follow my heart and my inner guide.

I went to the spring and began to drink from it. You might have heard about the famous water of Dhulikhel, but to try it for the first time is unique and rare. You understand the power of that water as you drink it; it is beyond anything one can imagine. The pure, crystal water of the Dhulikhel Himalayans water is unique. You can really feel that it is alive. It moves down inside your body in a torrent of energy carrying with it an unbelievable effect. You feel refreshed and reborn. You do not want to walk, but run, and jump; you feel completely empowered.

I sat there for a while watching the spring water sparkles dance between the stones. Suddenly, I felt a strange calling, a longing, a yearning desire coming from the surrounding area. I stood up and began to walk when, to my surprise, I saw behind me and to the left, a small opening into the mountain. I realized that there was a cave there. I entered the cave; it was like an irresistible magnet pulling me inside.

The cave seemed very familiar, as if I had been there long before. The impenetrable darkness inside it did not bother me at all. I touched the walls with a warm feeling of coming home after a long journey. The walls were surprisingly soft and gentle; the smooth surface was very pleasant to the touch. I caught a sweet fragrance of jasmine and rosemary coming from inside. I felt calm and serene.

Entering the Heart
the Way of the Third Eye

I intuitively felt a human presence inside the cave. It was not the movement of anybody in the impenetrable darkness that made me feel it, but a very powerful wave of energy coming from inside the cave. It conveyed a message to me and I knew that this message was coming from someone inside the cave.

Although I could not see anything in front of me, I stepped further inside trusting my intuition. After three or four meters, I stopped and felt a small bump in front of me. There was some kind of communication taking place between me and the space surrounding me, but it was happening inside me; it was not inside my mind, but somewhere in the area of the heart or maybe inside the heart itself.

It was as if there was an invisible speaker inside my chest broadcasting messages to me. Inside me, a clear and warm voice asked, in a very gently and familiar manner, that I sit on the small bump. I listened and made myself comfortable sitting in a half lotus posture. I realized that the bump was a big round stone with a small dent. It was a perfect stone for the half-lotus posture; I sat in the small dent cross-legged.

After few moments, I began to see the Master. Seeing in that place was in a completely different way from what I had been accustomed to. There were waves of different colors around us; especially green, blue, purple and indigo. Amongst the colors were infinite small sparkles of light. I felt as if I was suspended or floating in the universe amongst the stars.

In the middle of these waves and rainbows, I could sense, feel and see the outline of a body sitting in a lotus posture. Although it seemed as if the Master was floating in an ocean of colors and energy, I realized that he was sitting on a huge stone in from of me. The stone was clearly higher than my small bump, because his legs were at the level of my chest.

The Master spoke within me, through the "small speaker" from the area of my heart. I could clearly hear the voice inside me. Not a sound was uttered during my time in that cave. Our souls merged in an infinite vortex of energy and love. We travelled in worlds and universes that were far away, beyond our dimension. There was no time and space. We were united in the boundless and unlimited fields of Universal God. Then we felt the limitations of our bodies again. We were back in the cave feeling the energy around us.

We were grateful for Mother Earth allowing us such a great journey. We spoke for a while. The Master gave me a lot of answers to questions that had haunted me for a long time. Then he asked me to do a specific meditation that would help me stay in the heart. I will explain it all, step by step.

This meditation is not difficult at all; the only requirement, in order to have a similar environment like the one I had in the Himalayas, is to sit in a quiet place and turn off the lights. Darkness helps us move easily towards our heart and use our inner light.

First, you will need to close your eyes, even if you are in darkness, and start breathing rhythmically. While you witness the inflow and outflow of your breathing, allow your thoughts and concerns, your fears and issues to fade away. After few minutes, gently put your palms over your closed eyes gently allowing them to touch your eyeballs. The touch must be so gentle that you should almost not feel the palms over your eyes. The touch should be extremely light: like that of a feather or silk. It has to be as if not touching: it is more like a feeling. If you do it correctly then the energy begins moving within you. It begins to fall back inside you. It is like closing the door of your eyes when the energy begins to gather in that area; this is the area of the third eye. This is the area between your eyes or the middle of your forehead and the center of your brain; you will immediately feel lightness all over your eyes, face and head. You will feel as light as a feather, because the energy that falls back is moving within the area between your eyes and then it falls down into the heart.

You should feel as if you are levitating, as if there is no gravity. You should feel a light feeling entering your heart. Your whole body will relax and your breathing will slow down in sync with your heartbeat.

You should try keeping your palms over your eyeballs for at least half an hour. Remember that the whole issue is to maintain a light touch without pressing your eyeballs. Try to remember that your hands are weightless. If you can manage to do that for more than half an hour, your energy will flow constantly from the eyes towards your heart.

In the beginning, there will be only few drops, but if you practice continuously, each day for three months, then it will become like a waterfall flowing into your heart. This lightness will penetrate your heart and the heart will open. Remember that nothing heavy can enter the heart, only lightness. This lightness-energy from the eyes is like a waterfall pouring into the heart and the heart opens to it. In three months, you will be in the heart, and you will feel that you are floating into the center of the Universe.

Chapter 13

The Paradox

The journey had started a long time ago. Wondering into the infinite spirit, within my meditations, in the eternal cycles of reincarnations, I was able to see my never-ending efforts to enter and live in the sacred space of the heart. I went through all the methods written in this book and I practiced them with fervor and passionate unconditional love.

I have visited many places on beautiful Mother Earth, marveling at the unlimited ways the human spirit has to reconnect with the heart. I do not have a favorite way of entering the heart, although I do prefer the gentle methods of the feminine and intuitive energy. I do feel that especially as 2012, when Mother Earth had switched from masculine to feminine energy, we are bound to use the easiest way to connect with the heart, in the feminine way.

Ironically, although we are now living in the beginning of the feminine era, in some places of the world and different spiritual schools women are still not allowed to participate in the spiritual practices of the men. I have heard different explanations for this, but I believe that all of us should have the same opportunities and possibilities to practice all the methods that help us increase our level of consciousness.

Paradoxically, the majority of the methods used by men in the places where women are not allowed to participate are intuitive, feminine methods. This is a senseless contradiction of our natural way of living when the feminine energy today plays the most important role in our evolution. If we do not understand this truth and we continue to fight our nature, then we are bound to pay a huge price for it.

I have seen many practitioners all over the world, both men and women, following different spiritual practices and they do not allow themselves to embrace this new energy. Their work is full of obstacles, pain and suffering. The logic, male side of their nature, is keeping them in an artificial tension that will, sooner or later, produce an unbalanced and unstable field of energy around them.

The work for this book required my energy to be balanced and harmonized by feminine energy. I wrote the book in nature, connected with Mother Earth and my heart. Very often, animals and birds would gather around me as if I were part of nature itself. The trees protected me from the heat of the sun or the cold rain. I had a unique experience while writing Journeys into the Heart. I literally felt each method, as I was recollecting it.

Entering the Heart
Through Attention and Intention

I would like to give you one of the methods that I received while meditating with three Masters: *Thoth*, the Ascended Atlantean-Egyptian Master, *Anastasia*, the Siberian Great Master and *Babaji*, the immortal Mahavatar of Himalayas.

This method involves all the energy inside us: both male and feminine energy. It includes not just the heart, but also the brain and breathing. It has the qualities of all three Masters: the wisdom and knowledge of Thoth, the power and energy of Anastasia and the gentleness and Mastery of Babaji.

First you need to find a comfortable posture where you can keep your back straight, but without tension.

Relax your three points of tensions: the eyebrows, the shoulders and the hips.

Close your eyes and start breathing rhythmically.

Begin by observing your breathing without any interference from your part. Just notice the in-breath and the out-breath without altering it.

Then relax your head and let your chin gently go down towards your chest. Focus your attention on the frontal lobe of your brain for 3-4 seconds.

Then move your head to your left shoulder in the direction of a quarter of a circle until your left ear is over the left shoulder. Focus your attention on the left side of your brain for 3-4 seconds.

Move your head backwards as if looking up towards the sky. Focus your attention for 3-4 seconds on the back of your brain, on the occipital area.

Move your head towards your right shoulder until your right ear is over it. Focus your attention on the right side of your brain for 3-4 seconds.

Then move your head back to the first posture where your chin leans towards the chest completing the last quarter of the circle. Focus your attention again on the front side of your brain for 3-4 seconds. Then straighten your back and focus on the center of the brain.

Repeat this procedure 12, 24 or 36 times.

Now watch your breathing, its inflow and outflow and command your breath to slow down. Literally watch your in-breath and out-breath and command it "slow down", "slow down," "slow down"…

After a few seconds your breathing will slow down and you will be able to hear your heartbeat either as a sound or a sensation in the body.

Listen to your heartbeat carefully and imagine that your heart has split into four parts: front, left, back and right. Also feel the center of your heart in the middle of these four parts.

Now listen or feel your heartbeat, and at each heartbeat place your attention on each one of these four parts together with the center of your heart and repeat on each part the Tibetan Soul Mantra: *I Am Pure Love and Bliss; I Am in Light and Peace* in the following manner:

When you feel the first heartbeat, place your attention on the front side of your heart and say inside of you the word

I. Imagine the letter inside the front part of your heart; see it there!

Feel the second heartbeat, place your attention on the left side of your heart and say the word *Am*. Imagine the word "Am" inside the left part of your heart.

Now feel the third heartbeat, place your attention on the back of your heart and say the word *Pure*. Imagine the word "*Pure*" inside the back part of your heart.

Feel the fourth heartbeat, place your attention on the right side of your heart and say the word *Love*. Imagine the word "Love" inside the right side of your heart.

Now feel the fifth heartbeat and place your attention again on the front side of your heart. Mentally say the word *And*. Imagine the word "And" inside the front part of your heart.

Feel the sixth heartbeat and complete the first part of the movement focusing your attention inside your heart, between these four parts, right in the center of the heart, repeating the word *Bliss*. Literally see the word "Bliss" in the center of your heart.

Continue this exercise with the second part of the mantra, *I am in Light and Peace*, following the same procedure.

After twelve heartbeats, repeat this procedure until you have begun to feel warmth and lightness in the center of your heart. After half an hour or one hour of doing this meditation, depending on the time you have available, you will literally drop inside your heart, right into the center of the four parts of your heart. Then, as the three Masters told me, you will find who you really are.

Chapter 14

The Battle with Yourself

A special part of my life is daily dedicated to what I love tremendously: practicing Martial Arts. Beyond the black belts that I acquired over years of practicing, beyond the medals and the trophies that I won in competitions as a teenager, there is something that still continues to drive me to practice these techniques. You might think that Martial Arts are all about fighting, but besides the routine, more importantly than the hours and hours of sweat, the practitioner undergoes a change

I am grateful to all my teachers and Masters that helped me understand that martial arts is an inside battle. If you know yourself and manage the flow of energy towards the right direction, then you became a Master.

It starts with physical exercises; hundreds and thousands of repetitive movements; movements of hands and legs, of the lower body and the middle body, of the head and the neck. Movements that move your muscles and line of training towards a specific direction: learning how to defend yourself and counterattack with the application of the most efficient techniques.

It had become like dancing with a partner; but in martial arts your partner is not an enemy. He or she is actually the best friend in the world, because they are able to show you how to correct your errors.

Then after years of practicing, the Master gradually introduces the spiritual part: the meditation that comes at the end of the training. After hours of movements and sweating in the *dojo,* you get the best of it: a few minutes of meditation when you literally feel as if you are in the eye of the hurricane. All the tiredness and turmoil has gone; you are now settled in peace and calmness. Suddenly, you feel the vortex of energy around you; you are now in the center of the circle.

You are able to watch yourself and everything around you from the position of harmony and love. You direct the flow of energy in any direction you feel will benefit you.

I strongly advise parents to allow their children to practice martial arts or at least some martial art exercises. Tai Chi Quan, for example, involve movements that help strengthen the internal organs: the heart, liver, lungs, spleen, etc. A list and explanation of each movement and organ can be found on my website[3].

It is not about fighting, but about knowing ourselves. It is an inner battle: if you can win that battle, the outside challenges will settle in a very elegant way.

Martial Arts create a healthy mind: the famous zen *koan* metaphors are used by the great Masters in order to help practitioners see beyond a private opinion of one person or of one group. It is a way to test the student's understanding of a principle or of a fundamental truth.

---

[3] www.danielmitel.com/tai-chi-forms/

Last but not least, Martial Arts involve creating a healthy life; there is no Master in Martial Arts that does not embrace a healthy life. All Martial Art practitioners are in touch with Mother Earth and the universe. They are able to easily recognize our Cosmic Parents.

Entering the Heart
the Way of Doing Nothing

Have you ever tried to just sit, doing nothing, in silence and peace? You might think that it is easy, but Za-Zen Masters say that, in-fact, this is the most difficult thing to do in the world! After Martial Arts training where practitioners are completely exhausted, they practice the meditation of Doing Nothing.

They sit in complete silence, keeping their back straight and their eyes half-opened, allowing their gaze to gently rest ahead of them. They rest their hands, one over the other (men keep their left palm over their right palm and women keep their right palm over their left palm), with thumbs gently touching and forming an oval shape with the edge of the palms. They can stay in this posture from a couple of minutes up to one hour or even more than that.

Their awareness is focused on nothing; they just remain receptive and vigilant in the actual moment, in the now.

Try to do this meditation. This exercise is particularly difficult because thousands of thoughts, hundreds of arguments and fights pass through our mind. You will be reviewing your life again, through all the issues that you have gone through that bother your existence. Then, after few months of practicing this, you will feel sleepy and begin to dream, despite your eyes being half-open, gently gazing ahead of you.

You might dream, hallucinate or sleep. You will ask yourself why you are wasting time doing this nonsense exercise. Your ego will try to convince you how ridiculous your are, how pathetic all your attempts and efforts are. Your mind will laugh at you and you might get disappointed. You will get lost in memories and issues.

But do not give up! Continue this exercise. You must continuously try to be vigilant and in the moment. One day your mind and your ego will give up. They will become tired of you and they will give up the idea of catching you. On that day, all your energy will drop down into your heart and, suddenly, when you are simply sitting there, doing nothing, you will enter godliness, bliss and peace. That whole river of thoughts will disappear and you will be living in the moment, inside your heart.

Chapter 15

Dreaming in the Dream

I have extensively written about the Tibetan Masters and my time spent with them in my previous books, *This Now Is Eternity*, and *Heart Imagery: A Path To Enlightenment*. One of the most intriguing and enthralling topics, largely discussed in the books, is about dreaming and the dreaming state. I had experienced many "lost days" which I was unable to recall. However, somewhere, deep inside of me, I was aware that they were not really lost. All these vague memories were half-hidden there, waiting for me to reach a level of full consciousness that would reveal them to me. I knew that I was in a dreaming state, on a much higher level of consciousness.

Both Masters, Karma Dorje and Tenzin Dhargey, were not just controlling the dreaming state; they were Masters in a peculiar state of awareness called "dreaming in different worlds". What I understood is that this is the most complex state of awareness human beings can reach.

One of the interesting things that the Masters had told me was that a woman can use her dreaming body much easier than a man. According to the Masters, this great deal of fluidity comes from the fact that for a woman, in general, it is much easier to break ties with the past.

The Masters were experts at shifting levels of awareness. They could shift my awareness just with their presence. One moment we would be in what we call an awakened state and a moment later we would be in a dream state. It took me a while to absorb this new state of awareness, but once I had achieved it, I was able to dream in the dream state.

It is nothing like falling asleep into a dream. It is something more complex than that. The Masters consider that we are all dreaming now. Even when we wake up in the morning and we believe we are awake, we are still in a dream. So their goal was to make us become aware of the fact that we are dreaming.

The best way to do that is by arriving to a higher level of consciousness: dreaming in the dream.

They used two methods: either their simple presence would instantly shift my level of consciousness into the dreaming in the dream state or we would all simply go into a meditative state and work the presence of our dreaming bodies from that state of consciousness.

However, there is another method that they taught me, a method that can be practiced by anyone.

Entering the Heart
the Way of Dreaming

Whenever we would use the dreaming in the dream method, we would always focus our attention on the heart. Dreaming from the heart requires a great deal of attention, because in dreaming the whole nature of reality is different from what we believe it to be. Once we achieve the state of awareness given by our dreaming bodies, than all our solid assumptions will be gone.

The best way to understand this method is to practice what the Masters called "the knowledge of the heart". Almost similar to the system practiced by the Mystics from Mount Athos, this way of entering the heart requires tremendous attention and intention. The knowledge of the heart is an exercise that must be practiced all the time regardless of the hour of day or night or the activity we may be doing.

The intention is to keep the concentration in the heart and the attention must be focused only on the heart. As our minds have been conditioned to be practical and only accept what is verifiable and quantifiable, it is easy to practice the knowledge of the heart for a couple of minutes, even for an hour. According to Karma Dorje and Tenzin Dhargey, this is the first contact with our intuitive knowledge. Intuitive knowledge brings us flashes of insight and understanding.

However, if the exercise is not done constantly, doubt and forgetfulness arise because our minds and ego fight for their "rights". Once we are able to establish a constant connection with our heart and keep our intention and attention only on the heart, we are able to ascend to a higher level of consciousness: dreaming in the dream.

This consciousness develops gradually into our dreams. As soon as we are able to keep our intention and attention only on our heart, we become conscious of dreaming and reality becomes fluid around us.

This method requires a tremendous amount of attention because we need to be prepared to take the leap into the unknown. I could always feel the presence of both Masters when I was dreaming in the dream; it was as if they were allowing me to play in the unknown, but they were still there, somewhere around, watching me.

Because perception takes place at a point outside the body and the senses, this method opens a wide range of possibilities and arouses within us an extraordinary amount of energy. Advanced practitioners of the Dreaming in the Dream method are able to completely detach from the social order without retreating from the world.

Chapter 16

The Melchizedeks

Various distinctive cosmic teachers have been sent here to help and guide us and the Melchizedeks undoubtedly play a crucial role in the history of our planet. Legends lost in ancient times speak about Father Melchizedek, Machiventa Melchizedek, and the Twelve Council of Melchizedeks who were in charge of the goodwill of our planet. Some ancient texts make clear references to Machiventa Melchizedek, King of Salem, the priest of the Most High God.

As far as our understanding can go, Machiventa Melchizedek was the first Melchizedek who had bestowed himself upon the human race. Machiventa Melchizedek assumed the assignment of service as a mortal ascender being, allowed a temporary visit on Earth at Salem in the days of Abraham with the aim of helping and assisting humanity. He volunteered himself to come and help us and did so with the approval of the Twelve Council of Melchizedeks, who feared that life would disappear during that period of increasing spiritual darkness.

The second bestowal of a Son from the Melchizedek order happened in our modern times, when Drunvalo Melchizedek assumed another important assignment on our planet.

Who are the Melchizedeks and why do we whisper their names with such respect and devotion? According to the Mystics, the Melchizedeks play a large part in the education and training of all the celestial beings in our Universe: angels, seraphim, etc. They are not just teaching corps. Their activities also have to do with the supervision of our progressive ascending course. While the Melchizedeks are devoted to the educational and experiential training in our local universe, they also function in unique missions and in unusual situations. For this reason we sometimes call them "the emergency Sons".

The Melchizedeks are always trained to serve in any unusual circumstances, at any place in the universe. Whenever there is a situation or special help is needed, one or more Melchizedeks are ready to serve. They take action in any planetary crisis in any emergency of any nature in all worlds. They occupy an important part of the universe, a pilot world that is the first in a circuit of worlds, each of which is devoted to specialized activities. These worlds are often referred to as the Melchizedek Universities. Ascending beings from all over the universe pass through the Melchizedek Universities as part of their education. The pilot world, named the Melchizedek world, is regarded by all beings as the most interesting place in our universe.

TEACHING TOGETHER WITH DRUNVALO AT THE COSMIC GRACE WORKSHOP, MARCH 2015

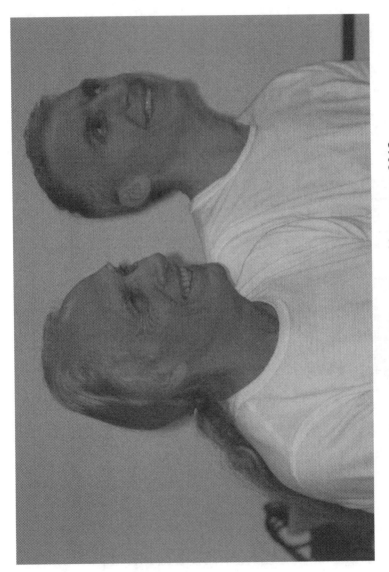

DRUNVALO MELCHIZEDEK AND DANIEL MITEL, JANUARY 2012

Chapter 17

The HeartMath Institute®
Expanding Global Hearts

Having read about the journeys of the heart in the Himalayas and Tibet, at Mount Athos, Sierra Nevada, as well as in other places of the world, one may ask if any scientific research conducted has been done that would show us how to improve our lives with the hidden power of the heart.

There is no better team in the world than HeartMath® that demonstrates the intelligence of the heart. The HeartMath® Institute was founded by Doc Childre in 1991 with the aim of assisting individuals, organizations and the global community to use and incorporate the intelligence of the heart into everyday experiences. By connecting science with the heart, the HeartMath® Institute empowers people and teaches us how to build our resilience levels, reduce stress. It provides ways of unlocking our inner guidance in order to make the best choices for ourselves.

The goal is to create a heart-connected world and for the last 25 plus years, HeartMath® has been developing and delivering scientifically based tools and technologies that help people connect their heart, mind and emotions and experience a greater sense of flow in their life, as well as reduce their stress levels.

A great initiative of HeartMath® Institute is the Global Coherence Initiative (GCI), created to promote peace and harmony, as well as activating humanity's core, its heart. GCI is involved in groundbreaking research on the interconnection between humanity and Earth's magnetic fields and energetic systems . As a Global Coherence Initiative Ambassador, I actively promote their studies and initiatives. As people experience more and more restlessness, overwhelm and energy drain, GCI has committed itself to creating global solutions. Scientists are studying the effect of the resonant frequencies in the Earth's magnetic field and how it influences human health and behavior.

GCI's hypothesis is supported by scientific findings showing that there is a link between the Earth's magnetic field and living systems. It is known today by scientists that the Earth's resonant frequencies are similar to those of the brain, the heart and the autonomic nervous system.

GCI is showing people the relationship of health and behavior with the solar and geomagnetic activity in order to help them understand the importance of a coherent heart-based human connection. By creating these kinds of coherent connections we will be able to transform and improve our world and the consciousness of humanity.

The Power of the Heart

Below is an interview of Agathi Christodoulidi, a HeartMath® Trainer, Teacher at the School of Remembering and co-founder  of the Motivate-Yourself organization. Agathi is a Master teacher, speaker, workshop facilitator, trainer and coach providing unique and outstanding programs for individuals, as well as for companies and executives.

As a HeartMath® trainer, Agathi also uses biofeedback devices of HeartMath® in her trainings and coaching. One of her main focuses is to train people on how to be aware of their emotional state and how to be able to self regulate.

As a co-founder of the School of the Heart, Agathi is dedicated to helping people all over the world in remember who they really are.

Do we have a hidden power inside of our hearts?
Our heart is one of the most interesting and mysterious organs of our body. Much has been researched about it, but it still cannot be fully understood. HeartMath® Institute has been researching the connection between the heart and the brain

for the last 25 years and has brought amazing information and new understanding about how the heart works and how it is influencing our psychophysiology.

In numerous ancient writings and techniques they speak about the heart, but only in recent days has science been able to figure out some of the importance and intelligence of the heart. For example, it is now scientifically proven that the heart generates an electromagnetic field that is bigger than the electromagnetic field of the brain.

Actually, as the Director of Research of the HeartMath® Institute, Rollin McCraty, wrote in the article, *The Energetic Heart: Bioelectromagnetic Communication Within and Between People:* "The heart generates the largest electromagnetic field in the body."

Information that has been intuitively known to ancient cultures and traditions is starting to be accepted and absorbed in our modern way of living. The notion that people should only follow a logical way of thinking and decide their lives based on logic alone, is fading as people see themselves grow into unhappiness and their life becomes all the more stressful and demanding.

People are beginning to look for different solutions and different ways of living their life and from my understanding and experience the easiest way to do this is to go back to the beginning, to return to our place of wisdom, to go back to our hearts.

Magnetic Field of the Heart

Our thoughts and emotions affect the heart's magnetic field.

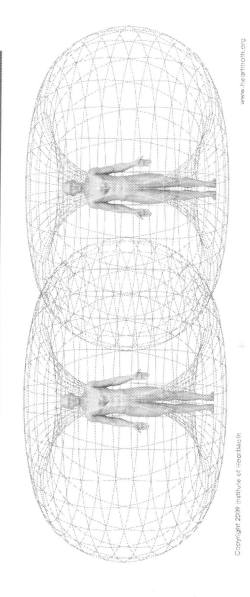

www.heartmath.org

Can we connect the heart and the mind and have a better way of living?

HeartMath® Institute has been exploring for years how the heart and the brain communicate and it has established that the heart can influence perceptions, emotions, intuition and health.

Research has shown that the heart communicates with the brain in four ways, neurologically (through the transmission of nerve impulses), biochemically (via hormones and neurotransmitters), biophysically (through pressure waves) and energetically (through electromagnetic field interactions). By knowing this, we can also safely assume that the more we listen to both, heart and brain, the better we will be able to obtain a more harmonious way of living and a better and balanced life.

Balancing and harmonizing the communication between the heart and the brain brings us in a state of increased focus, increased performance, emotional stability and overall improved wellbeing. When you are in such a state, which HeartMath® Institute calls "heart coherence", then you are able to act on the situations that happen to you instead of reacting to them. You become more gracious and understanding as you are in a state of harmony and peacefulness.

For example, think of the times you came home from a hard day at work, feeling tired and the only thing you wanted to do is relax. Now, remember how you reacted or how you felt when something happened that did not allow you to relax. It could have been something in the house that needed fixing or chores you had to finish, addressing the needs of the family and so much more that are a part of our busy and demanding everyday life.

In contrast, think of the times you came home from a pleasant day at work, when you were appreciated and praised for something, or when you had the day all to yourself and you did only the things you enjoy; on those days you went home feeling happy, relaxed and accomplished. How did you act to situations that had to be resolved or to that problems that had to be addressed?

Establishing a balanced connection between the heart and the brain allows you to be able to act accordingly on any situation that arises. It allows you to choose how you want to handle it instead of repeating patterns of outburst or anger. It also builds your resilience, so that you are in a better position to come back from any frustrating situation and to find "your peace".

It is essential for all to learn to exist in such a state of heart coherence, it is the only way were you are able to create your life in a balanced and harmonious way and chose the steps you need to take wisely in order to have a fulfilling and happy life.

What is the effect of love, appreciation and gratitude?

Emotions can affect the connection between the heart and the brain, as they change the activity of the Autonomic Nervous System. It has been understood since the 1960s that the way our heart communicates with our brain changes the way we view our environment and our surroundings. When we perceive a threat, the sympathetic nervous system is responsible for the body's "fight or flight" response and when we are at rest the parasympathetic nervous system is responsible for this function.

Research shows that different emotions affect the heart rhythms in different ways. For example, when we are experiencing "negative" emotions such as anger and frustration, then these emotions increase the activity of the sympathetic branch of the nervous system and they cause chaotic heart rhythms.

On the other hand when a person is experiencing love, appreciation or gratitude there is an increase of activity on the parasympathetic branch of the nervous system which creates smooth heart rhythm patterns.

"Positive" emotions, such as love, appreciation or gratitude generate cortical facilitation, thus improving our capacity for increased performance, focus, mental and emotional stability, clear thinking and more energy.

HeartMath® brings us great scientific discoveries about the heart and the intelligence it contains. Do we have a "brain in the heart"?

One of the findings of neurocardiology is that the heart has a complex neural network that could be characterized as "the brain of the heart" as it is sufficiently extensive and sophisticated. As Dr. Armour explains, the heart's nervous system contains around 40,000 neurons, which are sending information to the higher centers of the brain that influence perception, decision making and more cognitive processes.

Taking this into consideration, a new world of possibilities opens up and we now know that our heart also "thinks" or has a mind of its own! Since our heart also has the biggest electromagnetic field around our body the information that are being sent to our brain are much more diverse than the information that the brain receives on its own. This could be also the reason why in most ancient traditions the heart is considered to be so wise and they teach how we should be listening to its messages closely.

Can we create now a happier, healthier and more balanced life if we fully use the whole capacity of the heart?

During my workshops and trainings I have found that the more people start to understand the idea of an intelligent heart and allow themselves to listen to their inner knowledge and the messages that stem from there, they start to experience their life in a more fulfilling way.

I have seen people taking the steps they were hesitating to take for so long, after they truly realized and accepted that it is ok for them to trust and to listen to their heart. The mistrust that has been created in our society in not including our whole being in taking decisions and creating our life is starting to shift, as we now understand and know scientifically that there are other protagonists in our bodies and not just our brain. By allowing ourselves to work as a whole, to be balanced and synchronized we are able to think clearly, to act in harmony and to be in a constant state of coherence.

Moreover people learn to co-exist better within the business environment as well as their family life. Creating a state of peacefulness and a constant connection between your brain and your heart allows you to "hear" deeper thoughts and ideas that until recent you did not listen or you just ignored. A coherent state of being allows people to be in touch with their intuition, to be able to have breakthroughs in solving problems and to "download" new ideas, to be pioneers!

In a world that it is repeating itself, where old patterns are constantly at play the biggest need is innovative thinking, fresh ideas, new designs and breakthroughs. People can only have these when they are open to listening their inner voice and unfortunately stress, anxiousness, frustration and similar emotions and states, block our inner and intuitive thoughts.

The notion of a different world, a better way of living and a harmonious state of existence for all humanity can come only from each individual's ability and willingness to be in a more balanced state of being and a coherent way of existing. The accumulation of each one of us being in this state, will slowly, slowly, create a different energy, a stronger and better field where all of us will be living happily and in peace with ourselves and the people around us.

A very useful exercise that can be done by all people independent of age is HeartMath's Heart Focused Breathing technique. This technique will help you re-establish a harmonious connection between the heart and the brain and to balance your Autonomic Nervous System. It is a simple exercise that you can practice throughout the day while driving your car, prior a meeting, before going to bed or when you wake up in the morning.

Heart-Focused Breathing™ Technique

1. Focus your attention on the area of the heart. Imagine your breath is flowing in and out of your heart or chest area, breathing a little slower and deeper than usual.

2. Suggestion: Inhale for 5 seconds and exhale for 5 seconds (or whatever rhythm is comfortable). Your breathing should be smooth and comfortable. The more you practice the easier it is going to be to have an unforced and smooth breathing.

3. In the beginning try to put your hand over your heart as it will help you direct the focus to your heart.

For more information, please visit Agathi's websites[4].

---

[4] www.agathi.net/, www.motivate-yourself.org/, www.heartmath.org/

List of Meditations

ENTERING THE HEART

Meditation 1

The Unity of Breath Meditation
from page 5

Within a short time, Sri Yukteswar appeared to me with a noble expression on his face. Though I have had a close relationship with Yogananda, Sri Yukteswar's disciple, I had never really thought about Sri Yukteswar himself. But there he was. He went directly to the point, as I will now.

He told me that, in India, no one would even consider approaching the divine without a certain state of mind and heart, and he gave me very specific instructions on exactly how to consciously connect to the divine and finally with God. Here is what he told me.

You can be anywhere, but I use an altar with a single candle to focus my mental attention. I feel and know the presence of my teachers, and we all begin to breathe together, as one.

"Let your attention shift to a place on Earth that you feel is the most beautiful place in the world. It could be anywhere - a mountain scene with trees, lakes and rivers; or an arid, sandy desert with almost no life - whatever you perceive as beautiful. See as much detail as you can. For example, if your place is a mountain scene, see the mountains and the white, billowing clouds. See and sense the forest and the trees moving with the wind. See the animals—the deer and elk, little rabbits and squirrels. Look down and see the clear water of the rivers. Begin to feel love for this place and for all of nature.

Continue to grow into this space of love with nature until your heart is beating with the warmth of your love.

"When the time feels right, send your love to the center of the Earth using your intention so that Mother Earth can directly feel the love you have for her. You can place your love into a small sphere to contain it and send it to the Mother if you wish, but it is your intention that is so important. Then wait, as a child. Wait until Mother Earth sends her love back to you and you can feel it. You are her child, and I know she loves you.

"As your Mother's love enters your body, open completely, allowing this love to move anywhere throughout your body. Let it enter all of your cells. Let it move throughout your lightbody. Let it move wherever it wishes to move. Feel this beautiful love your Mother has surrounded you with and remain in this union with Mother Earth until it feels complete.

"At the right moment, which only you can know, without breaking the love union with your Mother, look to your Father, to your Heavenly Father. Look to the rest of creation beyond the Earth. Place your attention on a night sky. See the Milky Way as it meanders across the heavens. Watch the planets and the Moon swirl around you and the Earth. Feel the Sun hidden beneath the Earth. Realize the incredible depth of space.

"Feel the love you have for the Father, for the Divine Father is the spirit of all of creation, except the Divine Mother. And when this love becomes so great that it just cannot stay inside you any longer, let it move into the heavens with your intention. Again, you can send your love into the heavens inside a small sphere, if you wish."

Sri Yukteswar says to place your love in a small sphere and with your intention send it into the heavens. He says to send it to the unity consciousness grid around the Earth. If you do not know what this grid is, then do not worry. Just do as most of the indigenous peoples of the world do: send your love to the Sun. Like the grids, the Sun is connected to all the other suns or stars and eventually to all life everywhere.

Some people, such as the Hopi of the Southwest of the United States, send their love to the Great Central Sun, which is another concept that not everyone has but that is equally valid. Choose one — which one does not matter. The intent is for your love to reach all life everywhere.

Sri Yukteswar continued:

"Once your love has been sent into the heavens to the Divine Father, again you wait; you wait for the Father to send his love back to you. And of course, he will always do so. You are his child forever, and the Divine Father will always, always love you. And just like with the Mother's love, when you feel the love of the Divine Father enter your being, let it move anywhere it wants to. It is your Father's love, and it is pure.

"At this moment something that rarely happens is manifesting: the Holy Trinity is alive on Earth. The Divine Mother and the Divine Father are joined with you in pure love and you, the Divine Child, complete the Triangle."

According to Sri Yukteswar, it is only in this particular state of consciousness that God can be known directly. And so the final step in this meditation is to become aware of the presence of God—all around you and within you.

For this part of the meditation, Sri Yukteswar had originally given me a very complex way of being aware of God, but after speaking with many elders of various tribes around the world, I feel we can simplify the way to reach this final state of consciousness. It really is simple:

Once you are in the Holy Trinity, you can achieve this experience by simply opening your heart to the presence of God. For some reason that only God knows, in the Holy Trinity state the presence of God is easily perceivable.

Sri Yukteswar gave me the name of this meditation: the Unity Breath. God is always everywhere, but humans do not always perceive God. The Unity Breath meditation takes you directly, consciously into God's presence.

For some this state of consciousness is all that is necessary to complete all cycles created by life, or in another way of saying it, it is the doorway to approach all the sacred ceremonies of life, such as our birth into this world, sacred marriage and even death. According to the Native Americans, even the ceremonies of planting and harvesting crops require this particular connection to Great Spirit for the crops to grow and be healthy.

Different Ways of Entering the Sacred Space of the Heart

Meditation 2
The Kogi Way
from page 15

The Kogi, an indigenous tribe living high in the mountains in Columbia of South America, had shown me a way of entering the heart space. They would go into a totally dark space and "dance" a slow movement that seemed to have no direction. They would continue this dance without food, water or sleep for nine days and nights. According to the Kogis, at the end of this dance, they would be in their heart space.

DIFFERENT WAYS OF ENTERING THE SACRED SPACE OF THE HEART

Meditation 3
The Torus of the Heart
from page 15

I then had to find another way and knew that the heart created a huge magnetic field in the shape of a torus about eight to ten feet in diameter. It was believed that this field was generated by the Sacred Space of the Heart. I reasoned that if this is true, we could follow this field back to its source and find ourselves in the Sacred Space of the Heart. It works, and this is the first method that I had used. However, females have a hard time using this method. It is too logical.

DIFFERENT WAYS OF ENTERING THE SACRED SPACE OF THE HEART

Meditation 4
The Way of Jesus
from page 16

This way of entering the heart was first given to the world by Jesus. It came down through time by the Gnostic traditions. However, the Gnostics tried to hide this method from the public by saying that the Sacred Space of the Heart was not within the physical heart, but behind it. This is not true. But the entryway that Jesus spoke about is located behind the heart.

With this method, when you move from the brain to the heart, you move behind the heart and then turn and face in the direction you face when you are normally in your body. Now you are looking at the heart from behind. When you do this, you will see what looks like a crevasse or fold in the heart, and, in the middle of the crevasse, there is a small rotating vortex that appears either as a dark spot or a light spot. Move toward this vortex and, when you get close, the vortex will take you in, much like a vacuum cleaner, and you find yourself moving down a tube. Continue to move until you feel you come to a stop. At that moment, you are in the Sacred Space of the Heart. It is often referred to as the stillest place in the Universe.

DIFFERENT WAYS OF ENTERING THE SACRED SPACE OF THE HEART

Meditation 5
The Pure Female Way of Intuition
from page 16

This method is extremely simple, at least for females. For men it is a little difficult exactly because it is so simple. All you do is move from the brain to the physical heart and enter inside the heart from anywhere. Then with your intention, say to yourself that you are going to move and, when you stop, you are in the Sacred Space of the Heart. If you can use your female part of yourself, this is easy.

Different Ways of Entering the Sacred Space of the Heart

Meditation 6
Reconnecting with the Primordial Energy
from page 55

First you need to find a place to stay for at least half an hour. Get into a comfortable posture, keeping your spine straight and your eyes closed. Place your attention on the top of your head and imagine that you are inhaling the word "relax" through the fontanel, your crown chakra.

Then see yourself somewhere in the middle of nature, a place that you know and love and become part of the earth; feel, for example, that you have become a tree with strong and powerful roots. Then see that you are literally the earth; all five elements of the Universe are inside you: earth, water, wood, fire and metal.

Feel that you are getting bigger and bigger and the whole Universe is around you. Orbit around the Sun. Feel the connection with the thousands of stars around you.

ENTERING THE HEART

Meditation 7
The Intuitive Way
from page 60

C *lose your eyes,"* Lady Ana told us.

"See, sense and feel completely relaxed. Look at your mind and let it transform into a serene blue summer sky. It is as if you see it from below. All your thoughts are the white clouds moving across it."

We obeyed immediately. I noticed a calm and peaceful feeling.

"Let a gentle wind sweep all the white clouds towards the left until all of them have gone".

When the last cloud disappeared towards the left, an inner sound began to reverberate from the middle area of my chest.

"Feel or see where your heart is, or listen to the vibration that is coming from the middle of your chest. Listen to the sound of the heart and place your attention on it. It might be a vibration, a sound or the heartbeat," said Lady Ana.

In the beginning, I could clearly hear my heartbeat, the pulsation of the heart. Then the heartbeat began to fade and the vibration became stronger and stronger.

Intuitively, I followed the vibration and felt as if falling off a cliff. I almost became dizzy, but it was a very pleasant feeling. I was falling inside of me. I let it happen without resistance or anticipation. It was something irresistible that attracted me towards that direction, like a cosmic magnet.

Time and space became obsolete. I passed through thousands of stars and lights in just a few moments. Suddenly, I came to a stop. I did not stop in a compacted place It was a gentle end of the journey. . I could see colors, waves of light and energy. I could sense the presence of other beings. I could move freely as if there was no gravitation.

Lady Ana was quiet. Surprisingly, I could see her there near me, in that place where my spirit had arrived. It was not just her, as a human appearance; it was much more. Rivers of lights and colors abundantly surrounded her. She was enormous in a beautiful way. I felt calm and detached; there was something protecting me.

I could see anything through just my intention. I could move to any place in the Universe through just my intention. I could create anything through just my intention. I could communicate anything to anybody, anywhere.

ENTERING THE HEART

Meditation 8
The Way of Prana
from page 66

It is not my intention to initiate you to Kriya Yoga through this book, as this step takes the personal touch and supervision of a Kriya Master; however, I would like to share my experience of practicing the Kriya of the Heart.

Remember that, if we wish to achieve spiritual grace, we need to practice continuously; Lahiri Mahasaya's motto is *"Banat, Banat, ban jay!"* (Doing, doing, one day it is done!)

Some years of practice were sufficient to finally place my tongue in the Kechari Mudra, breathe rhythmically in Kriya Pranayama and begin a contemplative prayer.

After a while, my heart would start to vibrate continuously like a cosmic pulsar that emits regular light pulses. It is an inner calling that I cannot resist. It is like an interior magnet that attracts my undivided attention towards the heart. A warm feeling surrounds my chest and grows around my entire body like a protecting field of light.

I start moving inside my body like a spark of light inside the Universe. Sometimes it takes hours to cross space filled with galaxies and quasars, solar systems and stars into an infinite journey towards my heart.

Very often, I am still somewhere in the middle of the journey when I realize that three or four hours have passed and I need to get back into the day. I open my eyes and still feel a vibration in my whole body, especially in the area of the heart, for at least an hour or two.

Whenever I was able to cross time and space and arrive into the heart, I would feel born again. I would witness the great image of myself: pure, innocent and connected with Divinity.

Entering the Heart

Meditation 9
The Method of Simeon the New Theologian
from page 78

When practicing entering the heart with the Prayer of the Heart method, I extensively apply the method of Simeon the New Theologian. These instructions are clear and straightforward. Faith and patience are the main qualities required during this exercise. We must remember Master Lahiri Mahasaya's motto *"Banat, Banat, ban jay!"* (Doing, doing, one day it is done!)

I will first describe this method and then I will share my experience of doing it.

First we need to find a quiet place, a place where we meditate pray or do spiritual exercises. It is good to be in the same place every time because we charge it with a specific vibration that always helps us connect with our inner self faster.

Then we need to stop our thoughts. Simeon the New Theologian says that we need to withdraw our intellect from everything worthless.

The next step is to rest our chin on our chest and focus our gaze on the center of our belly or on our navel. Our attention must be fully concentrated on gazing at the center of our belly or our navel with no thoughts wondering around.

Then we need to calm down our breathing; we need to breathe really slowly and gently.

As we continue to practice gazing and breathing, we close our eyes and start to search for the place of our heart within us, where the Mystic says that all the powers of the soul reside.

In the beginning we will find darkness there and an impenetrable density. Later, as we continue to practice day and night, we will miraculously find an unceasing joy.

As soon as we find the place of the heart, the Master says that we will see things which we had been previously unaware of. We will see an open space within the heart that is entirely luminous and full of discernment. From this moment on, any distractive thoughts that may appear, will be driven away and immediately destroyed before they come into full fruition.

ENTERING THE HEART

Meditation 10
Nikiphoros the Monk, The Breathing Method
from page 81

Nikiphoros strongly suggests we find a Master or a Teacher that can guide us on the spiritual path so that we can arrive into the heart easier. He asks us to diligently and continuously search for a guide and if we do not find one then we must renounce our worldly attachments, call on God and start practicing alone.

As in the previous method, first we need to find a quiet place, a place where we meditate, pray and do our spiritual exercises. Again, it is good to be the in same place every time, because we charge that place with a specific vibration that always helps us in our practice.

Then, we need to concentrate our mind and lead it into the respiratory passage through which our breath passes into our heart.

We need to apply more pressure on our mind and compel it to descend with our inhaled breath into our heart. The Mystic says that, once the mind has entered there, it becomes united with the soul and fills with indescribable delight.

We need to train our mind not to leave the heart quickly, because, at first, it is strongly disinclined to remain constrained in this way. But once it gets used to staying there, it can no longer bear to be outside the heart.

Then all external things become irrelevant and peripheral. If, after the first attempts, we have managed to enter through our mind into the heart, we need to give thanks to God and continually persevere in this practice.

I really enjoy practicing this method. Before Nikiphoros, Buddha had used this method with his disciples. It is still used by Tibetan and Himalayan Masters. Buddha advised his students to practice it anytime during the day, but especially before falling asleep. It helps to dream from the heart and dreams become clean and uncontaminated by negative thoughts.

I like to practice this method in a quiet place; in the middle of nature whenever possible. Nevertheless, it can be practiced anywhere; sometimes I even practice during my flights while travelling and it works very well.

In the beginning, for a couple of minutes I try to feel my breathing pattern without changing it. I might breathe deeper or shallower and my breathing might even pause for a couple of moments. I just observe it without any intervention.

Then I try to let my mind follow the breathing flow, just as a leaf follows a waterfall. Sometimes, it is tricky because my mind tries to move away and escape the breathing flow. Indeed, as the Mystics have said, being watchful and vigilant, applying our attention and intention, is the key to success on the spiritual path.

After I have descended into my heart with my inhaled breath, I feel an inexpressible happiness and joy. My mind and my soul are unified and I am filled with peace and harmony.

I need to keep focus on my mind so that it does not leave the heart quickly, as, during this exercise, the mind has a tendency to leave the heart and move back into the brain.

Then all external things become irrelevant and I am completely detached and in peace. I always say a prayer and give thanks to God.

ENTERING THE HEART

Meditation 11
Nikiphoros the Monk, The Heart Concentration Method
from page 83

The Master asks that we use this method if, after having tried the breathing method as much as possible, we are still not able to enter the realms of the heart.

First we need to banish our thoughts and completely quieten our mind. Then we focus on the chest area, on the location of the heart and we start to repeat the prayer of Jesus ceaselessly: *"Lord Jesus Christ, Son of God, have mercy on me"*.

If we continue focusing on the heart and continuously repeat this prayer then, after some time, our heart will open and we will be able to easily use the first method, the breathing technique, so that we may enter the heart.

That is when, as Nikiphoros tells us, the whole choir of virtues - love, joy, peace and the others - will come to us.

I find this method very easy and pleasant to practice and the first time I practiced it, my mind had become completely quiet without any thoughts after just a few days.

This method is widely applied in India and in Tibet with the use of different prayers or mantras.

The Great Kriya Master, Lahiri Mahasaya, would use this method and changed the prayer according to the group of students he was teaching it to. Therefore, in one group of students he would use the Vasudeva Mantra, *"Om Namo*

Bhagavate Vasudevaya", while for another group he would use *"Lâ Ilâha Illâ Allâh"*.

I often use the Tibetan Prayer of love and peace: *"I Am Pure Love And Bliss; I am in Light and Peace"*.

Entering the Heart

Meditation 12
Nine Stages by St. Teresa of Avila
from page 85

This Master explains that there are nine stages of prayer, not nine different techniques as some practitioners are inclined to believe. Once we start the contemplative prayer we experience each stage as we arrive at that level of consciousness.

While using different methods of meditation, I was able to go into the heart in a natural way and, later, I could identify a specific stage from this Mystic's teachings.

These stages are:

1. Vocal Prayer
2. Meditation
3. Affective Prayer
4. Active Recollection
5. Infused Recollection
6. Prayer of the Quiet
7. Prayer of the Union
8. Prayer of Conforming Union (Ecstatic Union)
9. Prayer of Transforming Union

Below is a brief description of each stage, so that we may better understand how they can help us connect with our heart.

Vocal Prayer: St. Teresa of Avila recommends this stage for beginners of this practice. We choose the mantra or prayer that triggers in us much devotion and passion and we start repeating it. As the Spanish Mystic tells us, this is the door through which we enter the "inner castle."

Meditation After some time of preliminary vocal prayer, there is a stage in which we fight against distractions and disturbances. During this stage, we sometimes need to stop for a couple of moments and resume the mantra or prayer, until we find peace and peacefulness.

Affective Prayer: This is the stage where we find our hearts; we feel peace and kindness within. We can see, sense and feel inner light and inner vibration.

Active Recollection: This is the stage in which the prayer or mantra continues naturally; we feel as if in a trance and everything around us seems like a dream.

Infused Recollection: Here, we start to really feel the presence of God within us and around us; it is the stage where we feel divine grace entering our heart.

Prayer of the Quiet: This is the first stage of advanced prayer. Our memories slowly fade and we feel the intimate awareness of God permeating our soul and body. It is also referred to as the first stage of mystical prayer.

Prayer of the Union: Here, all our inner faculties are occupied by God; our memory and imagination are completely captivated by divine grace. The intensity of this mystical experience is beyond words.

Prayer of Conforming Union (Ecstatic Union): The last two stages, the ecstatic union and transforming union, are the last two degrees of mystical prayer. In ecstatic union, we feel as if we are on an ecstatic flight; sometimes, our body is literally lifted into space. Sometimes the soul goes out by itself; the experience is so profound that one never wants it to end.

Prayer of Transforming Union: Many Mystics identify this last stage of mystical prayer with "mystical marriage." It is the highest degree of perfection that one can attain in this life. It is a total transformation of the soul into the One. Divine love is totally expressed to us. The Mystics say that the Trinity, The Universal Father, Eternal Son and Infinite Spirit (The Mother), are fully experienced by our soul.

From the third stage up to the last one, the heart prevails. I was able to feel the presence of God inside me. The "recollection" is actually the remembrance of who I really am.

There are two different types of recollection and the Spanish Mystic attempts to give us a hint about each one. In the fourth stage, the active recollection, I almost felt numb, as if in a trance. Then, in the fifth stage, I was "infused" with divine grace, the infused recollection.

Words cannot describe the last four stages. These are mystical stages in which sometimes, for a couple of moments,

I would have a hint of what "mystical marriage" means, the union with the Divine.

In these stages, I would also feel a powerful, but ecstatic pain, within me. Sometimes I would be unconscious, almost fainting; sometimes I would remain without breathing for minutes.

My eyes would fill with tears and the experience was so intense that I almost felt as if an arrow had penetrated my heart. The pain would be sweet, but powerful; I would avoid eating, so as to prevent the experience from ending. I could stay in that stage all my life, just enjoying the divine grace in my soul.

ENTERING THE HEART

Meditation 13
The Heart Imagery Method
from page 91

One of the easier methods to go into the heart is the Heart Imagery Method. Prior to any imagery exercises, Masters, Karma Dorje and Tenzin Dhargey would give me a simple exercise to move me from the brain to the heart. They would tell me that this method is naturally experienced, especially by children.

Let's summarize this technique.

First find a comfortable position, keeping your spine straight and close your eyes.

Breathe out three times: draw in a normal breath and let out a long, slow exhalation through the mouth; as you exhale, see all your problems, issues, concerns and internal conflicts moving out and away. Then breathe in and out normally.

Now see, sense and feel that you are a big house. Imagine a room on top of the house; it is the room of the brain. A spiral staircase descends from the middle of this room (and the middle of your brain) to the middle of your chest.

Use your intention and go down the stairs.

When you arrive at the middle of your chest, step off the stairs and slowly turn to your left.

There is a door there that goes into your heart. It can be any type of door you imagine.

Open the door and step inside your heart; remember to close the door behind you.

Now see, sense and feel the power and love emanating from your heart.

If you read this method three-four times and then try to do it, you will be surprised at how easy it is to go into the heart.

I have few recommendations especially for the first time you practice this. First, once you are in the heart, you will see images, places, worlds and faces of known and unknown people. To be sure that you are actually in the heart and that it is not just your imagination, verify whether the light inside of the heart is polarized or non-polarized.

This is a very simple step. When the light is polarized, as it is in the brain, we can clearly see the shadows of the objects or the persons. This is because there is a source of light, which is the sun. Therefore, shadows are always caused by its light. However, the light in the heart is not polarized and there are no shadows.

ENTERING THE HEART

Meditation 14
The Natural Way of the Heart Chakra
from page 103

The intuitive way of the Heart Chakra begins, as mentioned in the previous chapter, with an intense clearing of emotional traumas and deeply distressing or disturbing experiences that have taken place in our lives. All the Masters I was blessed to meet and work with until now have said the same thing: the best way to clear these experiences is to forgive all the people with whom we have been in the conflict or disagreement.

It might be difficult and sometimes exhausting, but forgiving these people with whom we have been in friction clears all the survival negative emotions that keep our minds distracted by unnecessary energy-consuming thoughts.

When we feel that we have cleared the path and we have forgiven all the people with whom we have had a dispute or who have made us suffer, then we are ready to go into the heart using the intuitive way of the Heart Chakra of Unconditional Love.

The steps are easy to follow once we feel free of negative thoughts.

Basically we first need to move from the middle of the brain, where the Pineal Chakra is located, down to the Throat Chakra, at the base of the throat; then to the second Heart Chakra, that is located in the middle of the chest (the Chakra of Emotions) and finally down to the Heart Chakra of Unconditional Love.

From there we need to let our inner self or higher self guide us towards the heart. The physical heart is situated slightly to the left, in front of the Chakra. Therefore, we need to allow our attention to go in that direction. We also place a strong intention behind the attention and soon we arrive into the heart. Sometimes it takes many attempts to enter the heart, but after we have become accustomed to this method, it becomes really easy and natural to use it.

Entering the Heart

Meditation 15
The Heart of the Earth Method
from page 109

All aboriginal people know an ancient secret: if we connect with the heart of the earth, then we can enter our own heart in a natural way. They say that this is very easy to do.

The first step is to find a place in the middle of nature where you can relax, close your eyes and breathe rhythmically; a quiet place where you can hear the songs of birds and feel the breeze gently touching your skin. You might hear the sound of the spring water gently running into the valley or the sounds of waves touching the shore; any place where you feel relaxed and enjoy nature around you.

You might even be barefoot with your feet gently touching the ground or the grass. While you relax, keep your eyes closed and try to feel your heart in the middle of your chest. Slow down your breathing and listen to the heartbeat.

Feel your love for this place, for Mother Earth. Allow this love to grow inside of you. Then see, sense and feel a beam of light going down from your heart to the heart of Mother Earth, to the center of the earth. Allow all your love to go down through this beam of light towards the heart of Mother Earth. Feel and literally see waves of love and light travelling from your heart towards the heart of Mother Earth.

Place all your attention and intention on this process and soon you will feel Mother Earth' s response. It is like a warm cloud of light coming from below, entering first through your feet, then continuing up, penetrating each and every atom of your body.

This energy calms down all your thoughts and memories. You feel protected and safe from any danger. Your cosmic Mother helps and protects you. This powerful vibration might remain with you for hours, even for days if you love to be in nature or if you have activities in nature.

ENTERING THE HEART

Meditation 16
The Way of the Third Eye
from page 116

This meditation is not difficult at all; the only requirement, in order to have a similar environment like the one I had in the Himalayas, is to sit in a quiet place and turn off the lights. Darkness helps us move easily towards our heart and use our inner light.

First, you will need to close your eyes, even if you are in darkness, and start breathing rhythmically. While you witness the inflow and outflow of your breathing, allow your thoughts and concerns, your fears and issues to fade away. After few minutes, gently put your palms over your closed eyes gently allowing them to touch your eyeballs. The touch must be so gentle that you should almost not feel the palms over your eyes. The touch should be extremely light: like that of a feather or silk. It has to be as if not touching: it is more like a feeling. If you do it correctly then the energy begins moving within you. It begins to fall back inside you. It is like closing the door of your eyes when the energy begins to gather in that area; this is the area of the third eye. This is the area between your eyes or the middle of your forehead and the center of your brain; you will immediately feel lightness all over your eyes, face and head. You will feel as light as a feather, because the energy that falls back is moving within the area between your eyes and then it falls down into the heart.

You should feel as if you are levitating, as if there is no gravity. You should feel a light feeling entering your heart. Your whole body will relax and your breathing will slow down in sync with your heartbeat.

You should try keeping your palms over your eyeballs for at least half an hour. Remember that the whole issue is to maintain a light touch without pressing your eyeballs. Try to remember that your hands are weightless. If you can manage to do that for more than half an hour, your energy will flow constantly from the eyes towards your heart.

In the beginning, there will be only few drops, but if you practice continuously, each day for three months, then it will become like a waterfall flowing into your heart. This lightness will penetrate your heart and the heart will open. Remember that nothing heavy can enter the heart, only lightness. This lightness-energy from the eyes is like a waterfall pouring into the heart and the heart opens to it. In three months, you will be in the heart, and you will feel that you are floating into the center of the Universe.

ENTERING THE HEART

Meditation 17
Through Attention and Intention
from page 123

This method involves all the energy inside us: both male and feminine energy. It includes not just the heart, but also the brain and breathing. It has the qualities of all three Masters: the wisdom and knowledge of Thoth, the power and energy of Anastasia and the gentleness and Mastery of Babaji.

First you need to find a comfortable posture where you can keep your back straight, but without tension.

Relax your three points of tensions: the eyebrows, the shoulders and the hips.

Close your eyes and start breathing rhythmically.

Begin by observing your breathing without any interference from your part. Just notice the in-breath and the out-breath without altering it.

Then relax your head and let your chin gently go down towards your chest. Focus your attention on the frontal lobe of your brain for 3-4 seconds.

Then move your head to your left shoulder in the direction of a quarter of a circle until your left ear is over the left shoulder. Focus your attention on the left side of your brain for 3-4 seconds.

Then move your head backwards as if looking up towards the sky. Focus your attention for 3-4 seconds on the back of your brain, on the occipital area.

Then move your head towards your right shoulder until your right ear is over it. Focus your attention on the right side of your brain for 3-4 seconds.

Then move your head back to the first posture where your chin leans towards the chest completing the last quarter of the circle. Focus your attention again on the front side of your brain for 3-4 seconds. Then straighten your back and focus on the center of the brain.

Repeat this procedure 12, 24 or 36 times.

Now watch your breathing, its inflow and outflow and command your breath to slow down. Literally watch your in-breath and out-breath and command it "slow down", "slow down," "slow down"…

After a few seconds your breathing will slow down and you will be able to hear your heartbeat either as a sound or a sensation in the body.

Listen to your heartbeat carefully and imagine that your heart has split into four parts: front, left, back and right. Also feel the center of your heart in the middle of these four parts.

Now listen or feel your heartbeat, and at each heartbeat place your attention on each one of these four parts together with the center of your heart and repeat on each part the Tibetan Soul Mantra: *I Am Pure Love and Bliss; I Am in Light and Peace* in the following manner:

When you feel the first heartbeat, place your attention on the front side of your heart and say inside of you the word *I*. Imagine the letter inside the front part of your heart; see it there!

Then feel the second heartbeat, place your attention on the left side of your heart and say the word **Am**. Imagine the word "Am" inside the left part of your heart.

Now feel the third heartbeat, place your attention on the back of your heart and say the word **Pure**. Imagine the word "*Pure*" inside the back part of your heart.

Then feel the fourth heartbeat, place your attention on the right side of your heart and say the word **Love**. Imagine the word "Love" inside the right side of your heart.

Now feel the fifth heartbeat and place your attention again on the front side of your heart. Mentally say the word **And**. Imagine the word "And" inside the front part of your heart.

Feel the sixth heartbeat and complete the first part of the movement focusing your attention inside your heart, between these four parts, right in the center of the heart, repeating the word **Bliss**. Literally see the word "Bliss" in the center of your heart.

Continue this exercise with the second part of the mantra, *I am in Light and Peace*, following the same procedure.

After twelve heartbeats, repeat this procedure until you have begun to feel warmth and lightness in the center of your heart. After half an hour or one hour of doing this meditation, depending on the time you have available, you will literally drop inside your heart, right into the center of the four parts of your heart.

Then, as the three Masters told me, you will find who you really are.

ENTERING THE HEART

Meditation 18
The Way of Doing Nothing
from page 131

S it in complete silence, with your back straight and your eyes half-open, allowing you gaze to gently rest ahead of you. Rest your hands over each other (men left palm over right and women right palm over left), with your thumbs gently touching each other and forming the shape of an oval form with the edge of your palms. Stay in this posture for a couple of minutes up to one hour or even more than that.

Your awareness is focused on nothing; just remain receptive and vigilant in the actual moment, in the now.

Try to do this meditation. This exercise is particularly difficult because thousands of thoughts, hundreds of arguments and fights pass through our mind. You will be reviewing your life again, through all the issues that you have gone through that bother your existence. Then, after few months of practicing this, you will feel sleepy and begin to dream, despite your eyes being half-open, gently gazing ahead of you.

You might dream, hallucinate or sleep. You will ask yourself why you are wasting time doing this nonsense exercise. Your ego will try to convince you how ridiculous your are, how pathetic all your attempts and efforts are. Your mind will laugh at you and you might get disappointed. You will get lost in memories and issues.

But do not give up! Continue this exercise. You must continuously try to be vigilant and in the moment. One day your mind and your ego will give up. They will become tired of you and they will give up the idea of catching you. On that day, all your energy will drop down into your heart and, suddenly, when you are simply sitting there, doing nothing, you will enter godliness, bliss and peace. That whole river of thoughts will disappear and you will be living in the moment, inside your heart!

ENTERING THE HEART

Meditation 19
The Way of Dreaming
from page 135

The best way to understand this method is to practice what the Masters called "the knowledge of the heart". Almost similar to the system practiced by the Mystics from Mount Athos, this way of entering the heart requires tremendous attention and intention. The knowledge of the heart is an exercise that must be practiced all the time regardless of the hour of day or night or the activity we may be doing.

The intention is to keep the concentration in the heart and the attention must be focused only on the heart. As our minds have been conditioned to be practical and only accept what is verifiable and quantifiable, it is easy to practice the knowledge of the heart for a couple of minutes, even for an hour. According to Karma Dorje and Tenzin Dhargey, this is the first contact with our intuitive knowledge. Intuitive knowledge brings us flashes of insight and understanding.

However, if the exercise is not done constantly, doubt and forgetfulness arise because our minds and ego fight for their "rights". Once we are able to establish a constant connection with our heart and keep our intention and attention only on the heart, we are able to ascend to a higher level of consciousness: dreaming in the dream.

This consciousness develops gradually into our dreams. As soon as we are able to keep our intention and attention only on our heart, we become conscious of dreaming and reality becomes fluid around us.

This method requires a tremendous amount of attention because we need to be prepared to take the leap into the unknown. I could always feel the presence of both Masters when I was dreaming in the dream; it was as if they were allowing me to play in the unknown, but they were still there, somewhere around, watching me.

Because perception takes place at a point outside the body and the senses, this method opens a wide range of possibilities and arouses within us an extraordinary amount of energy. Advanced practitioners of the Dreaming in the Dream method are able to completely detach from the social order without retreating from the world.

THE HEARTMATH® INSTITUTE

Meditation 20
Heart-Focused Breathing™ Technique
from page 151

1. Focus your attention on the area of the heart. Imagine your breath is flowing in and out of your heart or chest area, breathing a little slower and deeper than usual.
2. Suggestion: Inhale for 5 seconds and exhale for 5 seconds (or whatever rhythm is comfortable). Your breathing should be smooth and comfortable. The more you practice the easier it is going to be to have an unforced and smooth breathing.
3. In the beginning try to put your hand over your heart as it will help you direct the focus to your heart.

About the Authors

Drunvalo Melchizedek

Few masters of our modern times have influenced our spiritual path as much as Drunvalo Mechizedek. He is the author of five

books: "The Ancient Secret of the Flower of Life": Volumes I & II, "Living in the Heart", "Serpent of Light" and "The Mayan Ouroboros." These books have been published in 29 languages and reach out to over one hundred countries throughout the world. Drunvalo has been featured on television and on the Internet, and has been written about in magazines, newspapers and books all over the world.

Having left the United States over 280 times, Drunvalo is a world traveler helping people understand their intimate connection to God.

Drunvalo is the first person in the world (in modern times) to have mathematically and geometrically defined the human light body, known in ancient times as the Mer-Ka-Ba. He is the founder of the Flower of Life Facilitators who teach his work in over 60 countries.

He has now founded his newest (and complete) teaching in a facility called The School of Remembering with the Awakening the Illuminated Heart Teachers who have begun their work on a global level.

Drunvalo graduated from the University of California at Berkeley with a degree in fine arts. He also has a minor in physics and math with only one quarter to finish his degree.

He lives in Sedona, Arizona with his loving wife Claudette and has six grandchildren.

Drunvalo created The School of Remembering to foster individual growth and increase the understanding of the human consciousness revolution that is now occurring. The School is a host to powerful eye, mind and heart changing experiences.

Health, peace and wellness are different experiences for everyone and the process can vary according to one's individual degree of awareness, personal vibration, spiritual practice and even individual purpose on the planet. We all have a calling and it's up to each of us to reach out and grasp our place in time.

Our happiness on a physical, mental and emotional or even spiritual level is about energy and consciousness. As one begins to experience new energies and new levels of consciousness, old patterns, behaviors, and beliefs that have limited one's perception and have kept their vibration in a denser state of being, begin to re-emerge.

Drunvalo helps people move past their own barriers and realize their own empowerment so they can remember and reconnect with their own place in the universe.

For more information, please visit his personal website[5]

Also by Drunvalo Melchizedek

  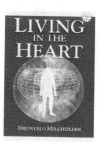

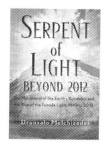 

---

[5] www.drunvalo.net

Daniel Mitel

Daniel is a world traveler Master helping people understand their intimate connection to their Inner Selves. He is the first

person in the world in modern times to explain and define the origin of the ancient Heart Imagery system. Heart Imagery, the ancient system that originates from ancient Tibetan, Sumerian and Vedic spiritual mystery schools, relates to the highest number of Mystery School: 555. It is related to Adamic Race, the power of dreaming and reversing the past, present and future.

Daniel began teaching teach Zen Meditation in 1981 and practiced the "spinal breathing" meditation between 1981 and 1992; later on he discovered that, in fact, he was practicing Kriya Pranayama of Great Master Babaji's Kriya Yoga.

Since 1996, he has been teaching Meditation Day Workshops and Heart Imagery Workshops worldwide.

Having spent a few years in meditation in north of Tibet, Daniel created "The School of the Heart" in 1999. Ten years later he created "The School of Meditation" in Toronto.

As an international lecturer and Martial Arts Master (Tai Chi Master and Karate Traditional Black Belt 5 DAN in WJKA – World Japan Karate Association), Daniel is dedicated to inspiring the world to shift from violence to peace and from anger to love. Through his work, workshops and spiritual conferences, Daniel has changed the lives of thousands of people.

He has an extensive academic background with a B.Sc. degree in Computer Engineering, B.Econ. (Hons.), Diploma in Management, as well as an MBA degree from the Open University Business School, UK.

As co-founder of Motivate Yourself organization, and in the role of a GCI (Global Coherence Initiative) Ambassador in the HeartMath Institute, Daniel actively provides training to companies all over the world.

The "Beyond the Limits" project with the UN Environmental Programme Goodwill Ambassador, Chairman and Pilot of SOLAR IMPULSE, Bertrand Piccard, represents a step forward in helping humanity move towards a cleaner environment, a better world, a better future.

Following his practice under the Tibetan Great Lama Masters, Daniel worked with a group of well known Masters from different schools of meditation (Osho, Dalai Lama, Babaji, Lahiri Mahasaya, Sri Yukteswar, Paramahansa Yogananda, Paramahansa Hariharananda, Paramahansa Prajnananda, Ana Pricop, Di Yu Ming, Sadhguru, Drunvalo Melchizedek, Anastasia) who train their students to be in the Heart.

Now, together with his own workshops, Meditation Day, Kriya Yoga (Spinal Breathing), Heart Imagery, Weekend with

Masters and Journeys into the Heart, Daniel also brings the Awakening the Illuminated Heart workshop to the world. Daniel had been appointed by Drunvalo Melchizedek in the first Awakening the Illuminated Heart (ATIH) Teacher's Council of the School of Remembering. In his capacity as Mentor, Daniel has helped and taught ATIH teachers from all over the world.

With these spiritual seminars, Daniel shares a message of hope and possibility to anyone who wishes to experience a new understanding of life; an understanding which comes from the heart.

Daniel has had the opportunity to work with Indigo Children from all over the world. He is blessed to be working with children, teaching them Tai Chi and Meditation.

Having being interviewed all over the world and constantly invited to write articles in magazines and on-line publications (Spirit of Ma'at, Collective Evolution, Vision, Lilou Mace, OMTimes and more), Daniel is one of the most prominent Meditation Masters known worldwide, showing the inner power that one can achieve using the Heart's unconditional love.

Daniel's books, This Now Is Eternity and Heart Imagery: a Path to Enlightenment, are highly regarded as some of the best meditation and spiritual guide books all over the world.

For more information about his books and his workshops, please visit his websites[6].

---

[6] www.danielmitel.com, www.heartimagery.org and www.motivate-yourself.org.

Also by Daniel Mitel

with BALBOA PRESS / a Division of Hay House

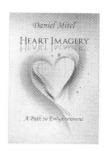

Printed in the United States
By Bookmasters